IMAGES
of America

BEL AIR

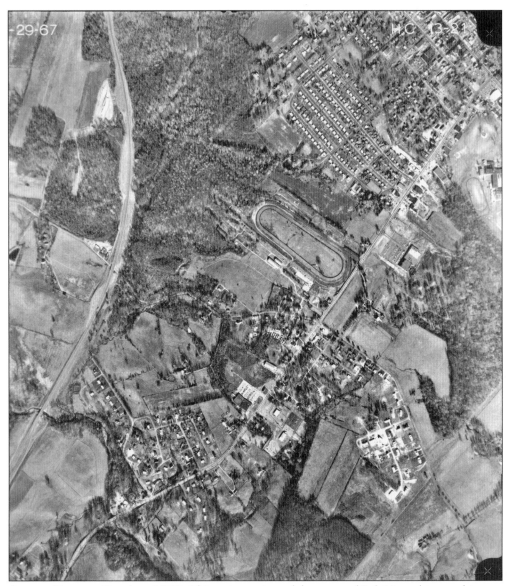

AERIAL VIEW OF BEL AIR, 1967. This unique view of the town of Bel Air and its outskirts on the west side of town reveals some landmarks even to the unfamiliar eye. Main Street runs along the very top right corner of the photo and goes quickly out of view. Below it and to the left of the downtown area are the neatly lined-up homes of Howard Park, one of the first housing developments in Bel Air, on what used to be the tomato fields of the farm at Liriodendron, the Kelly estate. Route 1 winds its way down from the upper right corner of the photo to the lower left corner. Bel Air High School is visible on the upper right side; the running track and baseball fields are wide open and easy to discern. Toward the middle of the photo is a shape similar to the school's running track, only it is much larger: the Bel Air Racetrack. (Courtesy Charles L. Lutz, Inc.)

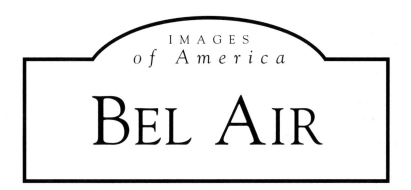

IMAGES
of America

BEL AIR

Bill Bates

ARCADIA

Copyright © 2004 by Bill Bates
ISBN 0-7385-1689-9

First published 2004
Reprinted 2004, 2005

Published by Arcadia Publishing
Charleston SC, Chicago IL, Portsmouth NH, San Francisco CA

Printed in Great Britain

Library of Congress Catalog Card Number: 2004107296

For all general information contact Arcadia Publishing at:
Telephone 843-853-2070
Fax 843-853-0044
E-mail sales@arcadiapublishing.com
For customer service and orders:
Toll-Free 1-888-313-2665

Visit us on the internet at http://www.arcadiapublishing.com

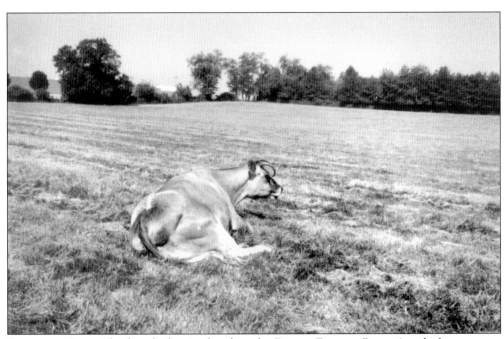

BETSY THE COW. This bucolic bovine lived on the Deaton Farm on Route 1 and often sat near the road just past the Bel Air Racetrack. Did she know she was the unofficial greeter for folks coming into Bel Air by way of Route 1? That's just how folks remember Betsy, Bel Air's landmark livestock. (Courtesy the Historical Society of Harford County, Inc.)

CONTENTS

ACKNOWLEDGMENTS

Dear Reader, I will begin by thanking you. If these photos and stories bring back happy memories of "good old" Bel Air, or if you're new to the area and these pages help you feel closer to your new home, then I have done my job. I'd love to hear from you: your reactions, suggestions, or your special Bel Air memories. You can reach me through my Web site at http://www.belairbook.com. You'll also find there added material, photos, and comments from other readers.

This book is composed of irreplaceable photographs. I would like to thank everyone again for the photos I have used and for those that I could not use, mainly because of space limitations. I appreciate their trust in allowing me to handle their cherished photos.

Thanks to those who have shared their memories and have helped bring to life the photos in this book. I have tried to share many of those stories in the photo captions.

Thanks to those who referred me to people or resources by suggesting contacts, making phone calls on my behalf, arranging meetings, and even accompanying me to see photos, places, or people in order to help my research along.

Thanks to those who graciously gave me their time when I dropped in unannounced, usually on a sudden hunch, or with a "quick" question. And thanks to those who expressed an interest in my project whether in a coffee shop, at the Bel Air Book Festival, or on the street as I took photos.

For their interest, help, and encouragement, thanks to David Andrews, Dennis Baxter, John Baxter, Kathy Casey and the folks at the Bel Air Book Festival, Jim Chrismer, David Cohen, Ronan Corbett, Dave Davis, Carolyn Evans, Pat Fielder, Ruth Foard, Dorothy Francis, Payson Getz, Mary Goodman, Jim Harkins, George Harrison, Mary Henderson, Mary Rose Isennock, Marcus Johnston, Neal Kennedy, Laura Lang, Lois Nagle, Richard Sherrill, Maryterese and Eugene Streett, Kathy Wajer, Craig Ward, John Worthington IV, Don Young, members of the Bel Air History Club, members of the Education Liaison Committee and board members of the Harford County Chamber of Commerce, and the Board of Directors of the Liriodendron Foundation.

Thanks to my editor at Arcadia, Susan E. Beck, for her encouragement, support, quick responses, and sweet Southern accent.

Thanks to Jim Welsh and Jeremy Rowan, Town of Bel Air, for their interest in and help with the project. Thanks to Maryanna Skowronski, administrator of the Historical Society of Harford County, and Richard Herbig, president of the society, for their support of this project. I especially appreciate their trust in allowing me to work so closely with the society's staff and resources. Thanks to Thirza Brandt for training me so well in using the society's photographic archives and especially for her memories and friendship. Thanks to the volunteer staff of the Historical Society of Harford County for their helpful suggestions, comments, and fellowship along the way. Some writers say that the craft of writing is a lonely art; I have rarely felt such camaraderie as I found at the society. Thanks to Matt Button of *The Aegis* for granting me access to the newspaper's files, and then going above and beyond by scanning the photos I had chosen, saving me quite a lot of time. Thanks to Bill Seccurro, president and CEO of the Harford County Chamber of Commerce, for his interest in the project and for allowing the Chamber staff to photocopy work to help with my research (and to Liz Jeppi for doing it quickly).

Thanks to my children, Geoffrey and Emily, for their love, humor, patience, and inquisitive spirit.

Thanks to my wife, Mary Ellen, for her unfailing love, confidence, and support.

INTRODUCTION

This book traces the changes and growth of the town of Bel Air through vintage photographs and the memories of its inhabitants. You will see the ghost of the past as you walk the town from Main Street's south end to its north end, over to Bond Street, which parallels Main, and then along the side streets and outskirts of town. As befits a town that has remained vital to Harford County and Maryland from its beginnings, Bel Air was made for growth and change.

Bel Air came into existence in 1782 as the seat of government for Harford County in a political coup that still ruffles some feathers today. Unconnected to the wealth and power of the port town of Havre de Grace on the Chesapeake Bay on the east side of the county, Bel Air was the creation of its developer, Aquilla Scott. Scott took some old fields in the middle of his vast land holdings in the county and marked off just enough land for a court house, a sheriff's house and jail, and a main street extending north and south of the court house in 42 half-acre plots like a Monopoly® board ready for play.

The new development, initially known as Scott's Old Fields, was named Bel Air after a suggestion by the Marquis de Lafayette, who was far more romantic than the literal Americans. Lafayette was one of many Revolutionary patriots and supporters who traveled regularly through the county. (His connection with the area is strong, and you may see his statue as you enter Havre de Grace—a tribute for his help in advancing the American cause against the British.)

Over the years, Bel Air grew and changed; Scott's land surrounding the small town was sold and resold for farms, dairies, mills, iron furnaces, iron factories, wheel factories, carriage factories, worker housing, churches, canneries, schools, a racetrack, car dealerships, shopping centers, housing developments, and more commerce and industry than Scott could have dreamed.

The properties and roads have developed over the years to adapt to the ever-increasing population. The small town of Bel Air was incorporated in 1874 and has increased in size to 2.9 square miles with a population of 9,722 folks comprising 4,235 households in the year 2000. The surrounding zip codes of Bel Air and all of Harford County comprise a bedroom community that continues to attract many urbanites to the beauty of the country just 23 miles north of Baltimore.

Bel Air has always granted easy access to the surrounding areas. It was part of the pathway of the National Road Project in the early 1800s. The posts outside the buildings of Main Street in early photos indicate transportation by horse and rider, buggy, carriage, and stagecoach. The National Road was abandoned for the speed of the Maryland and Pennsylvania Railroad, which brought city dwellers to build country homes or stay the summer at Bel Air's hotels. The milk and produce from surrounding farms were transported quickly into Baltimore by road and rail. The early paving of Route 1 spurred the improvement and development of other roads important to Bel Air's growth, especially Routes 7 and 40, and Interstate 95.

After a brief orientation in chapter one, you will time-travel through town in chapters two through six. Chapters seven and eight give you a glimpse of Bel Air's transportation, schools, and sports through the years.

A note on dating the photos: except for the images they contain, many photos do not have notes or identification indicating the date of the photo. Where such documentation exists, I have included the date in the boldface title of the photo caption. Otherwise, in the text of the caption, I mention possible dating according to evidence in the photos or from other records.

Although I have included as much information as possible in the captions, the text is not exhaustive; for more information about Bel Air, its places, and its people, please view the website that complements this book at http://www.belairbook.com.

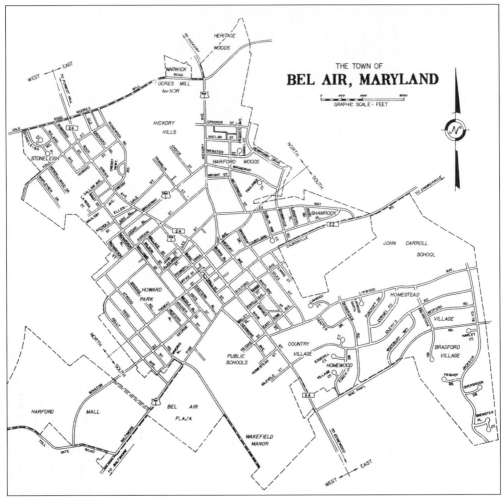

MAP OF BEL AIR, 1974. To help get you oriented for your tour of Bel Air, this 1974 map of the town is a good place to start. The dashed lines indicate the town limits. Only a few commercial properties and small housing developments have been added to the edges of town since 1974. The town increases in size when the owner of a commercial or residential development contiguous with town land requests to be accessioned by the town. If the request is approved, the landowner pays town taxes and other fees in return for town services. The greatest change to the map since 1974 has been the elimination of Wall Street behind the court house. The huge Masonic Temple located between Wall and Bond Streets was demolished to enlarge the court house back to the edge of Bond Street along Office and Courtland Streets. (Courtesy the Historical Society of Harford County, Inc.)

One
GETTING STARTED

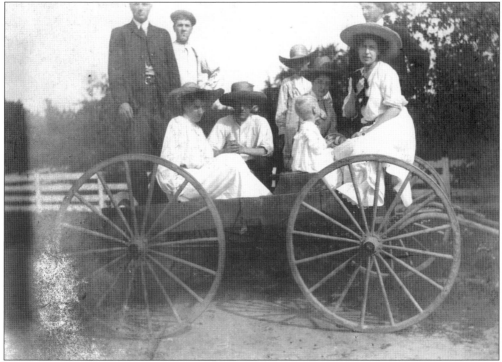

GROUP OF PEOPLE ON A WAGON. Even into the 1900s many folks in and around Bel Air used the horse and wagon as their primary mode of transportation. Perhaps these are dark-suited land owners and a tenant farm family. Note the light-colored clothing and broad-brimmed straw hats to keep cool in the heat of the sun. (Courtesy the Historical Society of Harford County, Inc.)

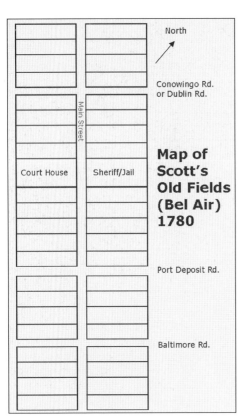

North

Conowingo Rd.
or Dublin Rd.

Map of Scott's Old Fields (Bel Air) 1780

Main Street

Court House

Sheriff/Jail

Port Deposit Rd.

Baltimore Rd.

MAP OF SCOTT'S OLD FIELDS. Although the street names and the orderly arrangement of lots have changed, the spirit of Aquilla Scott's original plan has kept the heart of Bel Air beating for over 200 years. This is a more or less central court house surrounded by shops, offices, and homes. (Author's re-creation.)

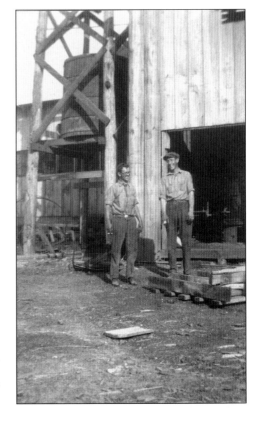

CANNERY WORKERS. Bel Air was well situated to become important to the area's canning industry. Farmers like Fritz Kelly grew acres of tomatoes to sell to nearby canneries to process, can, pack, and ship to other areas of the country, and especially to Baltimore, by way of rail and truck. (Courtesy the Historical Society of Harford County, Inc.)

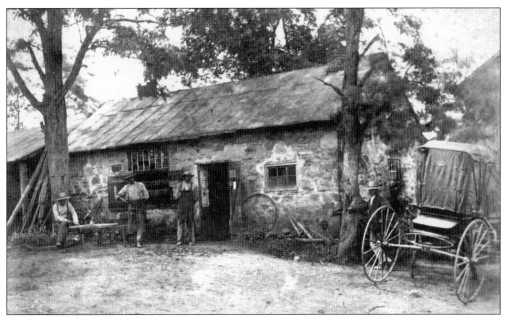

SMITHY. Iron production and iron working were a great part of the local economy. Various furnaces in the area, including the nearby Harford Furnace, produced iron for the smiths to fashion into farm and construction tools, wagon wheels, and other implements, such as cast iron frying pans, on which daily living depended well into the early 1900s. (Courtesy the Historical Society of Harford County, Inc.)

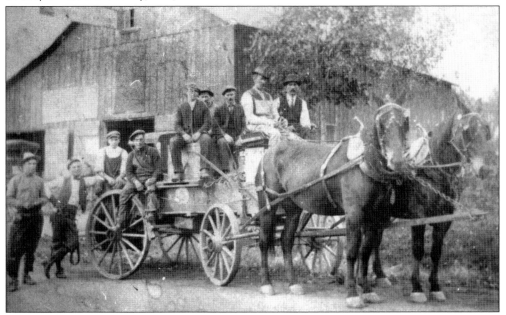

WORKERS WITH HORSES AND WAGON. The horse closest to the camera seems to be striking a pose along with the men. While the photo is too faded to read the sign on the barn-like building that seems to be the workplace of these men, the manner of dress, delivery, and décor (or lack thereof) is in keeping with pre-1900 Bel Air. (Courtesy Gene and Mary Streett, Boyd & Fulford.)

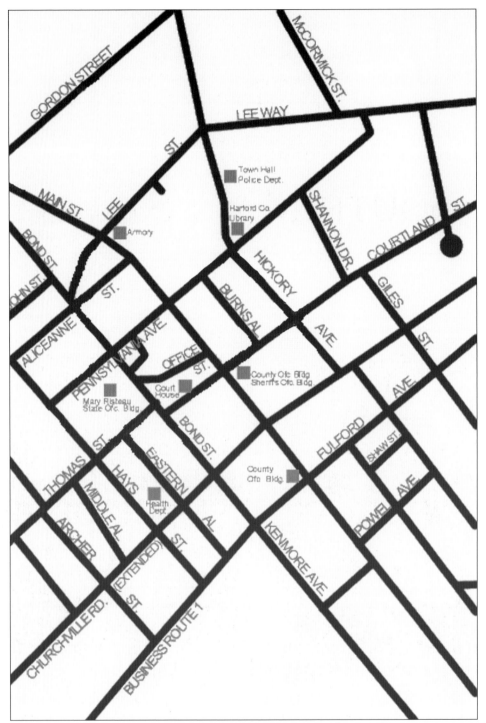

MAP OF DOWNTOWN BEL AIR, 2004. After a period of moving the new shopping centers and office complexes away from the downtown area, such establishments are moving back to Main Street as the prime location for doing business in Bel Air. There is a new appreciation of the town and its historic ambiance. (Courtesy Town of Bel Air.)

Two

ALONG
SOUTH MAIN STREET

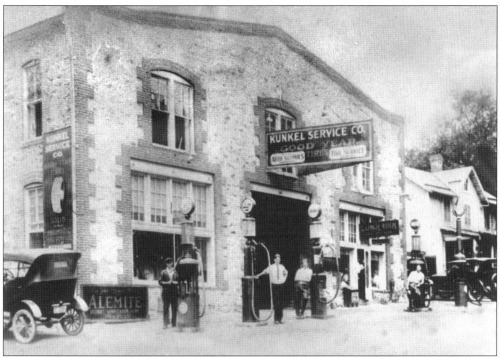

THE KUNKEL SERVICE COMPANY. Kunkel's 1920s stone building on Baltimore Pike between Bond and Main Streets would later be remodeled in brick and, later still, torn down with the adjoining home to make room for the Equitable Trust Bank. Eventually the bank itself was converted into the Harford County Government Office Building and parking lot. Note the Good Year sign advertising solid and pneumatic tires for sale. (Courtesy *The Aegis*.)

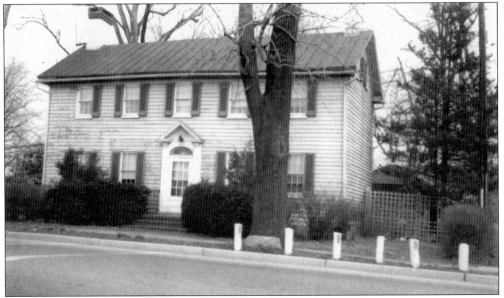

THE FULFORD HOUSE. This house stood on the southeast corner of Main and Baltimore Pike. Homes in Harford County are unofficially named after their first or most notable owners. This applies to historic homes and to homes in established neighborhoods. If Mr. Davis was the first to dwell in the home now owned by Mr. Smith, the house is probably still referred to as the Davis home. (Courtesy the Historical Society of Harford County, Inc.)

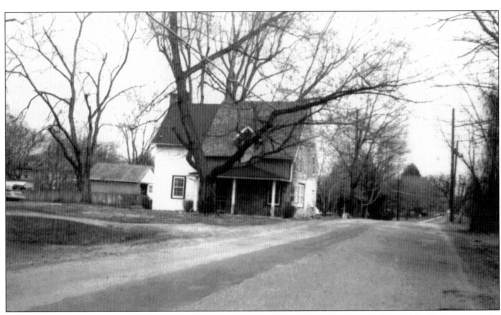

FULFORD COTTAGE. This cottage stands on the back end of what was the Fulford property. In the early 1900s the Fulford brothers made flavored syrup here for their soda fountain in the Boyd & Fulford Drug Store and made and bottled Lord Calvert soda for delivery to stores. John Schafer recalls lining up with other kids at day's end for the last drippings of syrup and soda. (Courtesy the Historical Society of Harford County, Inc.)

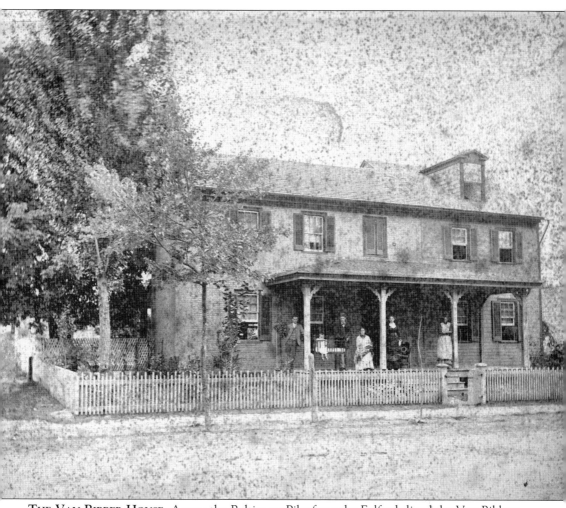

THE VAN BIBBER HOUSE. Across the Baltimore Pike from the Fulfords lived the Van Bibbers. The home was occupied by others before the Van Bibbers, but the notable family made an impression on the town, especially its last occupant, George Van Bibber, who was a bachelor and also a painter, writer, and man about town. In this undated (1880s?) photo, there seems to be a painting just inside the downstairs window on the left. Someone upstairs is making use of the shutters (no screens in those days). George's father, Dr. Van Bibber, would be on call at all hours. Active in the horse-and-buggy days, he would ride long distances to see patients. He knew he could depend on his horse to pull his buggy back home without guidance down the dirt road. The good doctor often fell asleep on the journey home. (Courtesy the Historical Society of Harford County, Inc.)

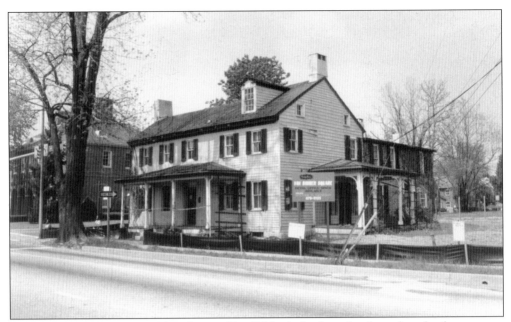

THE VAN BIBBER HOUSE. After George Van Bibber's death, a developer bought the property and hoped to move the historic homes at the Main Street/Baltimore Pike intersection onto the Bel Air High School grounds to form a mini historic Bel Air village. In the days before historic preservation made sense to others, the developer went broke with his dream unrealized. (Courtesy the Historical Society of Harford County, Inc.)

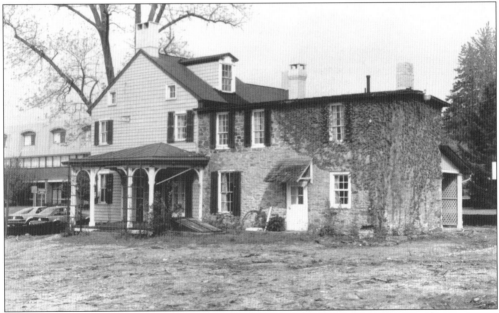

THE VAN BIBBER HOUSE. This view of the Van Bibber House in the late 1970s shows a stone addition to the dwelling. As of this writing the Van Bibber House, under a new owner, looks in poor repair with steel, glass, and brick offices attached to its sides like robotic arms on a Victorian mannequin. See photos at www.belairbook.com. (Courtesy the Historical Society of Harford County, Inc.)

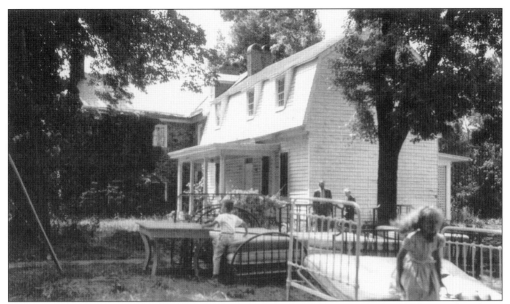

THE HAYS HOUSE. Almost a victim of the wrecking ball, the Hays House was moved in 1961 onto Bel Air High School property a block away to make room for a Safeway food store. In this photo assets from the home have been put outside for sale. Children are testing the durability of the beds. (Courtesy the Historical Society of Harford County, Inc.)

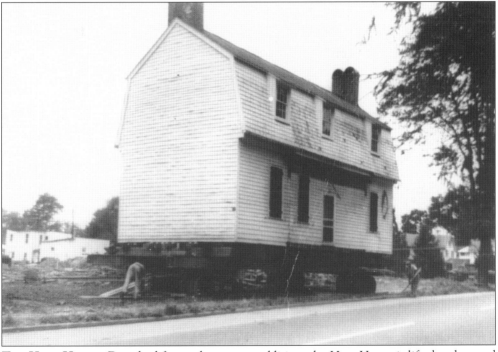

THE HAYS HOUSE. Detached from a later stone addition, the Hays House is lifted and moved to its new location and is today managed as a museum by the Historical Society of Harford County, which has added a kitchen in the spirit of the home's original kitchen. Docents often dress in Colonial fashion. (Courtesy the Historical Society of Harford County, Inc.)

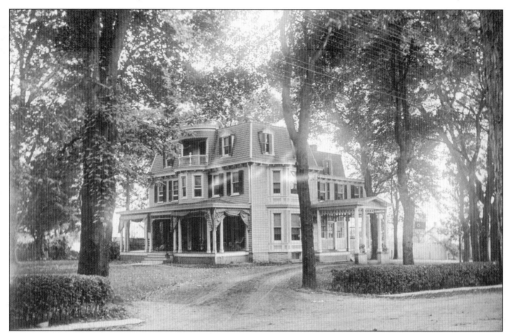

THE KENMORE INN. This rare photo is the proof copy of the original photo for a postcard of the Kenmore Inn. The leavings of horses on the road must have been so common as to be invisible to the photographer, who did not remove it from the foreground of the image. (Courtesy Gene and Mary Streett, Boyd & Fulford.)

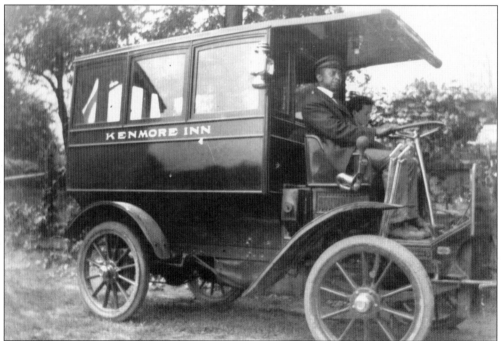

KENMORE COACH. Guests arriving by train at the Bel Air station were shuttled to the Kenmore by way of this horseless carriage. One of the competitors in town, the Eagle Hotel, met guests with a horse-drawn carriage. (Courtesy Gene and Mary Streett, Boyd & Fulford.)

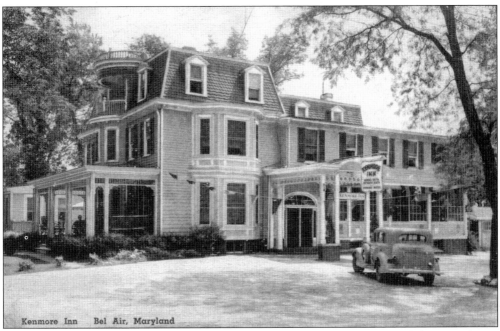

THE KENMORE INN. Postcards spread the word about an inn or hotel. Many of the Main Street shops also had series of postcards made featuring their storefronts and the attractions in Bel Air. The back of this postcard reads: "Kenmore Inn in Old Harford County Bel Air, Maryland. On Route 1 via Business Section. Rooms with Private Baths. Phone Bel Air 99. Good Food. Gift Shop." (Courtesy Lois Nagle.)

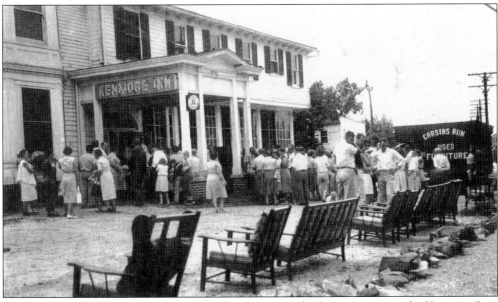

KENMORE INN SALE. Making way for the development of a shopping center, the Kenmore Inn, like the Hays House, is forced to put its furniture and contents up for sale. Unlike the Hays House, though, the Kenmore Inn would be demolished. (Courtesy the Historical Society of Harford County, Inc.)

19

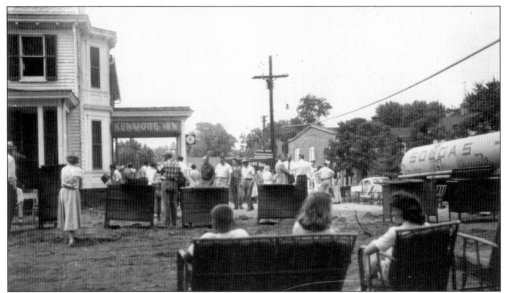

KENMORE INN SALE. More than just a tourist destination, the Kenmore was, in its heyday, the place for Sunday dinner in Bel Air. Lois Nagle remembers it fondly as the place of her first date with "Sparky," her husband-to-be, in November 1950. (Courtesy the Historical Society of Harford County, Inc.)

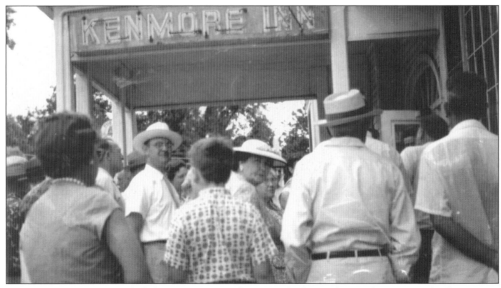

KENMORE INN SALE. While homes across Bel Air might have chairs, dressers, and other pieces of the old inn, part of the mantel from the famed fireplace is used as an antiques display in the window of the Boyd & Fulford Drug Store on Main Street. (Courtesy the Historical Society of Harford County, Inc.)

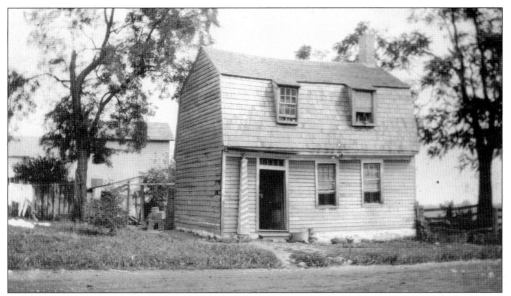

THE PINCKNEY HOUSE. William Pinckney had an office in this house during the time he was a representative to the Maryland legislature. The Harford delegation was the lone dissenting voice in a battle over legislation, favored by the wealthy, to increase taxes for working class citizens. These photos are from a photo album once in the collection of James Wollon, an architect who lives in Havre de Grace. (Courtesy the Historical Society of Harford County, Inc.)

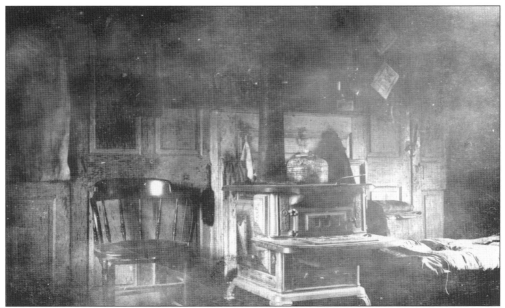

THE PINCKNEY HOUSE, INTERIOR. Wollon's album states: "The house in which William Pinckney first lived after his marriage to Miss Rodgers of Havre de Grace. This old house originally located where Kenmore Inn is now (1934) located at the corner of Main St. and the Bel Air Road was moved down the Bel Air Road opposite the end of Bond Street Bel Air. It was destroyed in 1912." (Courtesy the Historical Society of Harford County, Inc.)

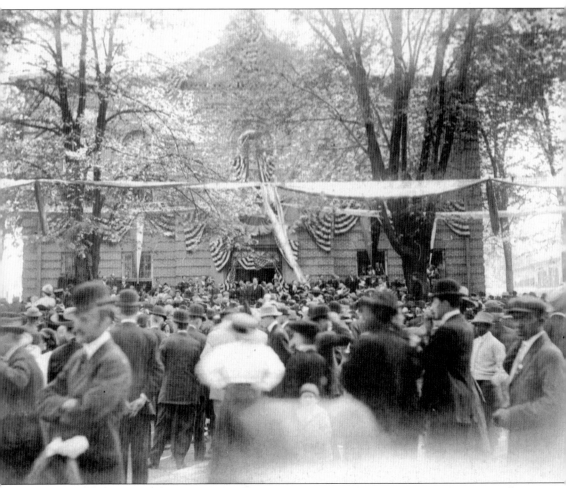

PRESIDENT TAFT AT THE COURT HOUSE, 1912. Toward the end of his presidency, William Howard Taft visited Bel Air. The town decorated shops and homes for the occasion. "Big Bill" Taft is in the center of the photo and passersby ignore the camera or look into it. (Courtesy the Historical Society of Harford County, Inc.)

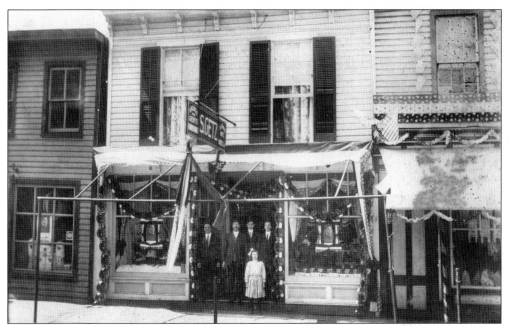

WAITING FOR PRESIDENT TAFT TO ARRIVE. Solomon Getz and his children stand in the doorway of their 26 South Main Street clothing shop, which is decorated for Taft's visit. Pictured are, from left to right, the following: (front row) Rebecca Getz; (back row) David Getz, Solomon Getz, Louis Getz, and Simon Getz. (Courtesy Payson Getz.)

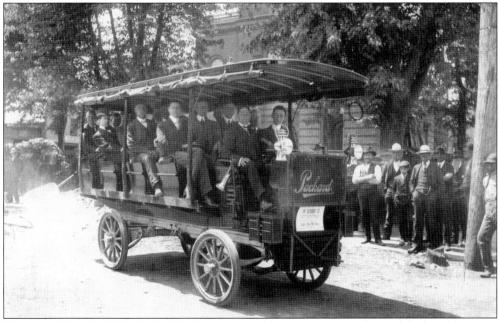

PACKARD BUS. In 1913, Bel Air's first motorized bus service carried city folk from the court house, down winding Harford Road, to the streetcar stop at Carney. From there the extensive Baltimore streetcar system would deliver them to points throughout the city. The express service was probably faster than taking the train. (Courtesy the Historical Society of Harford County, Inc.)

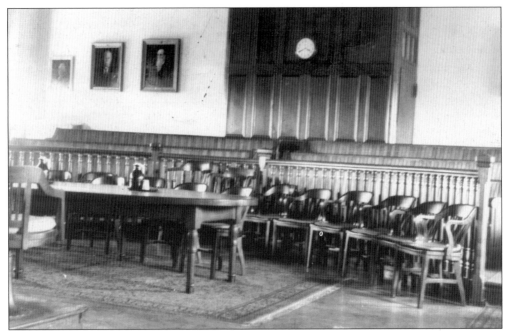

BEL AIR COURT HOUSE, INTERIOR. The original wooden court house burned down and was replaced by the sturdier brick version, which still stands. The oval table at which lawyers and clients sat during proceedings was saved from the fire. The table is still in use today. (Courtesy the Historical Society of Harford County, Inc.)

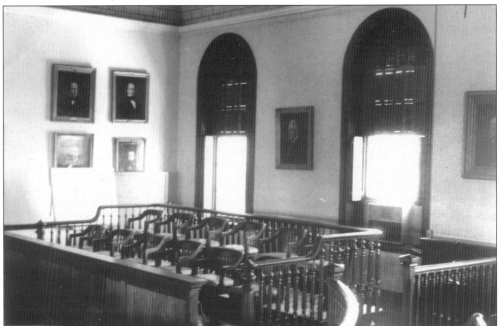

BEL AIR COURT HOUSE, INTERIOR. The jury box looks as uncomfortable as doing one's civil duty can be. Portraits of notable county citizens, as seen here, adorn the court house by the dozens. They lend a sense of continuing history to the building, which has been modernized except for this room. (Courtesy the Historical Society of Harford County, Inc.)

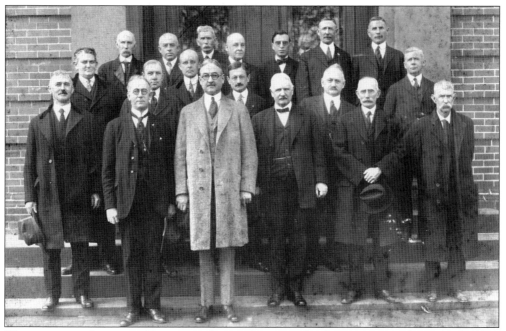

UNIDENTIFIED GROUP IN FRONT OF COURT HOUSE. The first court in Bel Air was held in Gilbert Jones's tavern. Jones rented quarters to the court before the original court house was built. The tavern was on the site of the James Broumel House (seen to the right of the Kunkel building on page 13). (Courtesy the Historical Society of Harford County, Inc.)

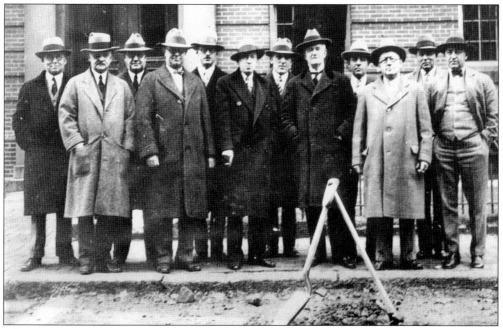

GROUNDBREAKING FOR SEWER SYSTEM, 1933. Pictured in front of the court house are, from left to right, the following: unidentified, Phillip Close, John Robinson, two unidentified, Simon Getz, Michel Fahey, Dr. P. Sappington, unidentified, Milton Wright, unidentified, Judge Ed. Harlan. Judge Harlan lived in the Broumel House mentioned above. (Courtesy Payson Getz.)

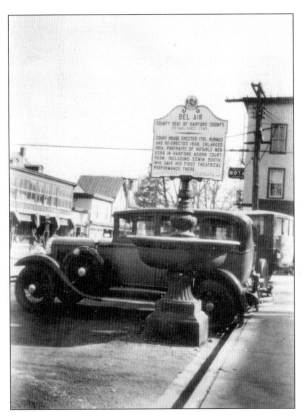

COURT HOUSE HISTORICAL MARKER. The marker reads in part: "Court House erected 1791. Burned and re-erected 1858. Enlarged 1904. Portraits of notable men born in Harford adorn Court Room, including Edwin Booth, who gave his first theatrical performance there." The Bel Air Rotary Club paid for the marker in 1930. The marker sits atop a fancy horse trough. (Courtesy the Historical Society of Harford County, Inc.)

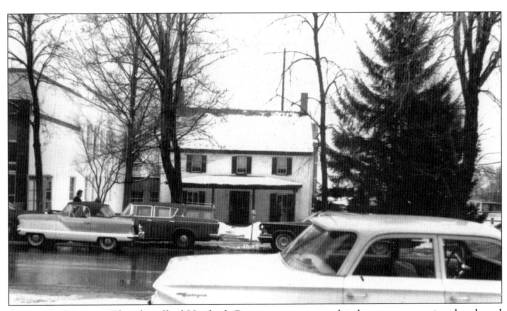

SHERIFF'S HOUSE. The sheriff of Harford County was given this home, conveniently placed across from the court house, to serve as his family's dwelling and as the jail. (Courtesy the Historical Society of Harford County, Inc.)

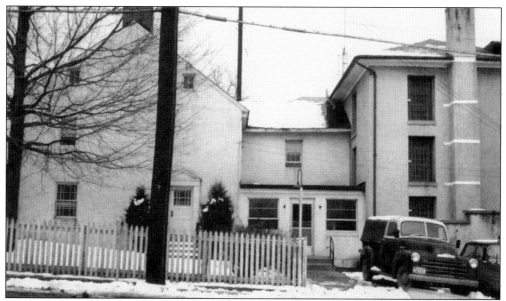

SIDE VIEW OF SHERIFF'S HOUSE AND JAIL. When the house was torn down to build the county's first modern office building (quickly outgrown), the jail, attached to the back of the house, was kept intact and integrated into the new structure. (Courtesy the Historical Society of Harford County, Inc.)

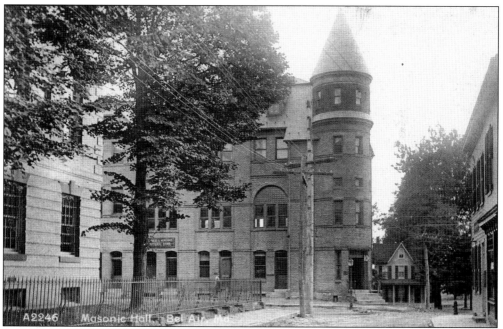

MASONIC HALL. This early postcard image of the hall, usually called the Masonic Temple, shows an ever-present feature of photos of Bel Air: phone and power lines criss-crossing in front of almost any view of the town. The temple sat behind the court house between Wall Street and Bond. Note the court house fence and Office Street storefront on the right. (Courtesy the Historical Society of Harford County, Inc.)

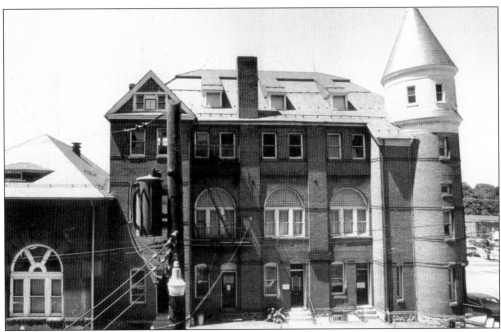

MASONIC TEMPLE, FRONT. What has changed from the previous view? The streets are paved, the cars are newer, some Bond Street homes and a hotel were replaced with a shopping center and car dealerships. Despite all the changes, the power lines are still there. (Courtesy the Historical Society of Harford County, Inc.)

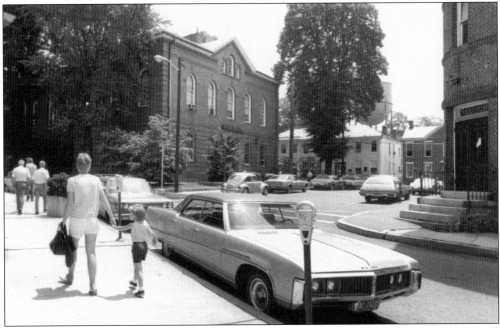

WALL STREET VIEW. Those shorts tell you these photos by Todd Holden were not taken all that long ago. To those who came to know Bel Air after the Masonic Temple was demolished in 1980 to expand the court house, this view must seem like something from an alternate universe. (Courtesy the Historical Society of Harford County, Inc.)

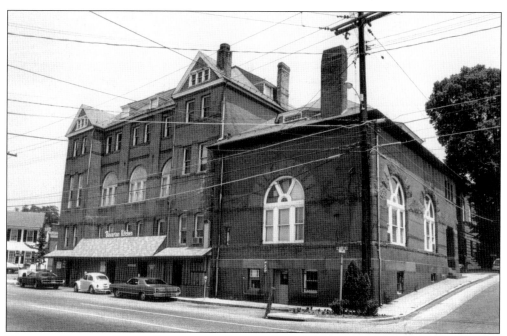

MASONIC TEMPLE, REAR, COURTLAND STREET SIDE. Like many buildings in Bel Air, one structure served a number of purposes. The front view shows the temple with separate office entrances and a blocky bank on the left. The rear view shows a restaurant and barber shop. In its day the temple rented its hall for meetings, conventions, church services, and other town occasions. (Courtesy the Historical Society of Harford County, Inc.)

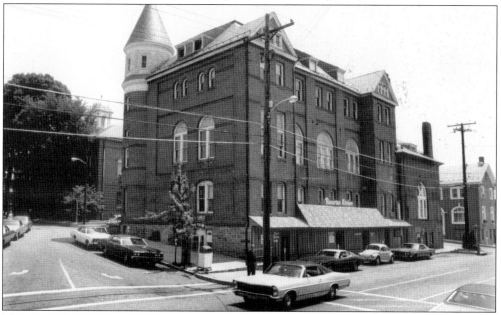

MASONIC TEMPLE, REAR, OFFICE STREET SIDE. Many of these photos are real treats for car buffs. Participation in civic groups has always been strong in Bel Air. A 1990s list of civic, volunteer, and non-profit totaled more than 700 such groups active in the county. (Courtesy the Historical Society of Harford County, Inc.)

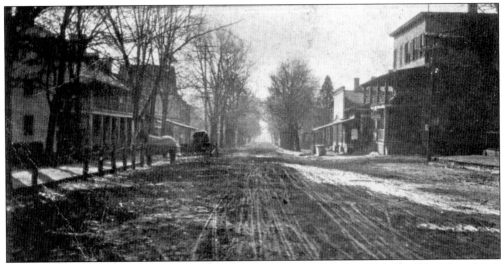

SOUTH MAIN STREET VIEW. The postmark on this postcard is dated July 11, 1907, but this is a winter scene featuring bare trees and a horse wearing a blanket. Frozen wagon wheel ruts stream out of the center of the photo and down Main Street. (Courtesy the Historical Society of Harford County, Inc.)

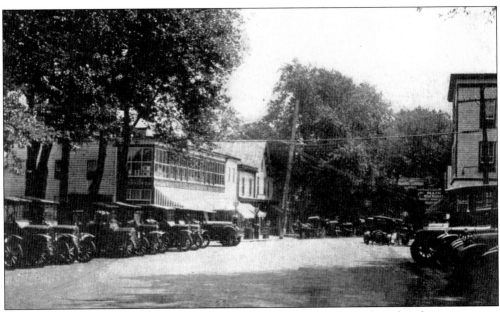

SOUTH MAIN STREET VIEW. This view of Main Street shows how slow the changeover was from horse to horseless. Roadsters line the street while horse-driven carriages are hitched to posts farther down the road. The hardware store at left would soon undergo some changes of its own. (Courtesy the Historical Society of Harford County, Inc.)

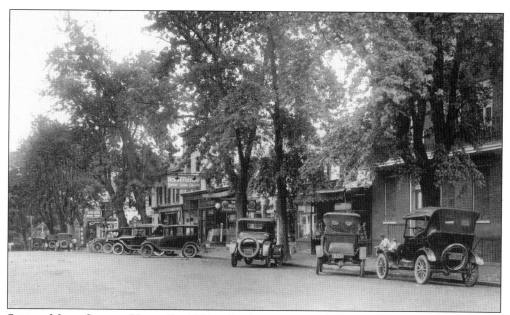

SOUTH MAIN STREET VIEW. By 1921 a few businesses, such as Boyd & Fulford Drug Store, settled in and become Main Street mainstays. F. Bond Boarman's hardware store changed ownership to become Courtland Hardware. Although it was remodeled and moved to Bond Street, Courtland Hardware is still part of the Bel Air business scene. (Courtesy Gene and Mary Streett, Boyd & Fulford.)

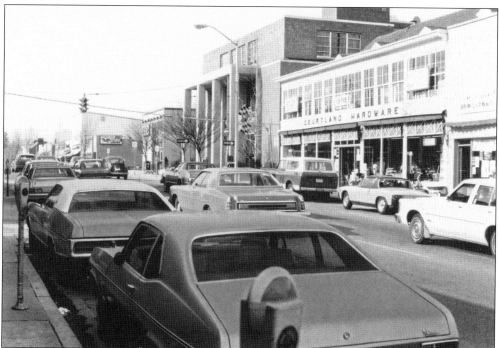

SOUTH MAIN STREET VIEW. This photo reveals 50 years worth of change on Main Street: the roads are paved, there are fewer trees, and traffic is one way (north). This is the view just before Main Street was repaved in 1979. (Courtesy Gene and Mary Streett, Boyd & Fulford.)

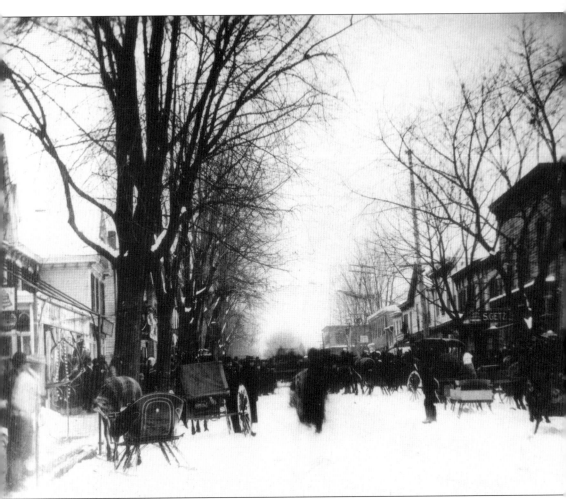

MAIN STREET WINTER CARNIVAL. In the horse-and-buggy days, when the snow was deep enough for a spontaneous horse-drawn sleigh ride, Main Street would close to traffic and hold the annual Winter Carnival. The main event was a sleigh race from the north end of Main Street all the way down to the Farm Fair area. On the right side of the photo is the sign for S. Getz, Solomon Getz's store. (Courtesy the Historical Society of Harford County, Inc.)

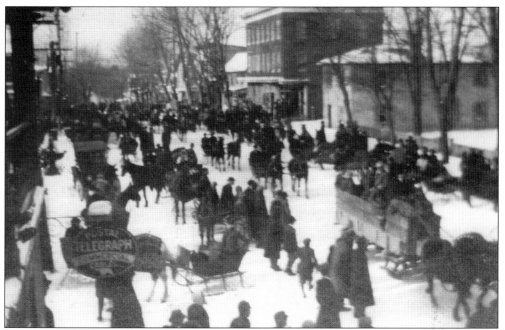

MAIN STREET WINTER CARNIVAL. Someone upstairs at the Stagmer Hotel has captured the jolly nature of the carnival, the whirling snow, and quick step of puffing horses. (Courtesy Gene and Mary Streett, Boyd & Fulford.)

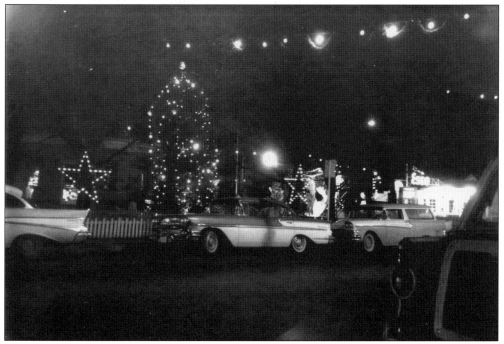

MAIN STREET HOLIDAYS. Nothing says Christmas in the 1950s like Chevys, Esso, and lights in series (one goes out, they all go out). Maryterese Streett recalls when Bel Air residents could do all their holiday shopping for clothing, jewelry, toys, tools, personal items, and even furniture on Main Street. (Courtesy the Historical Society of Harford County, Inc.)

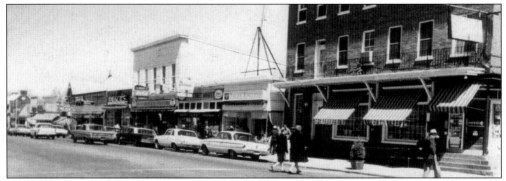

SOUTH MAIN STREET VIEW. In the 1960s many men are still wearing hats; they probably bought them at Hirsch's Men's Store. Main Street Market is still there, as is Boyd & Fulford's. Preston's Stationery is in the corner of the Vaughn Hotel, on the right. (Courtesy the Historical Society of Harford County, Inc.)

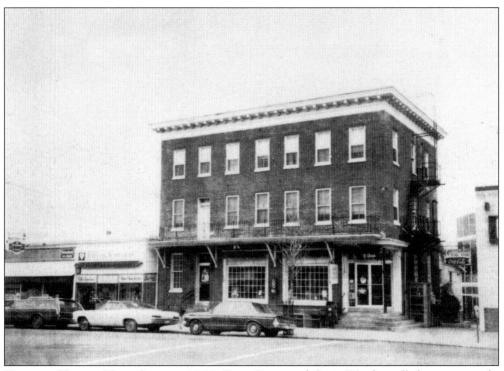

VAUGHN HOTEL, MAIN STREET, 1966. Dave Davis and Craig Ward recall the many nooks and crannies of the Vaughn Hotel. A below-street-level front entrance led to a barber shop. A side entrance led to a bowling alley, Poo-Poo's pool hall, and, later, slot-car racing tracks. Davis also remembers a movie theater, possibly the Harford Theater. That is a lot of entertainment in one package. (Courtesy the Historical Society of Harford County, Inc.)

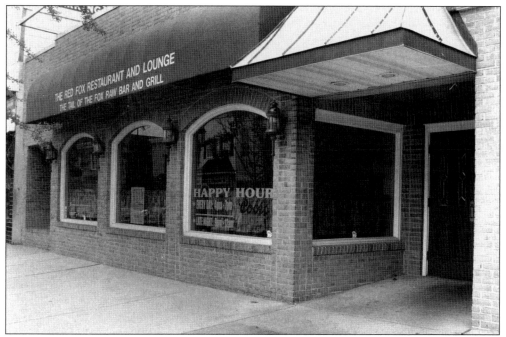

THE RED FOX, MAIN STREET. North of the Vaughn Hotel was the Red Fox Restaurant. This is the post-fire remodeling. The big fire of February 2, 1972, destroyed the Vaughn and damaged many of the nearby storefronts. It seems one cannot safely house an oil tank and a gas-fired heater in the same space. But then, the Vaughn was built before fire safety codes. (Courtesy *The Aegis*.)

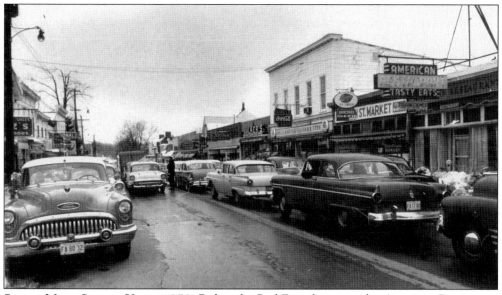

SOUTH MAIN STREET VIEW, 1958. Before the Red Fox, there was the American Restaurant. There were always plenty of choices for eating. The drug stores all had soda fountains. According to Dave Cohen, Mrs. Panos, who came to Bel Air in 1914, ran the Candy Kitchen, which really did start out making candy but soon became a burger joint. (Courtesy the Historical Society of Harford County, Inc.)

35

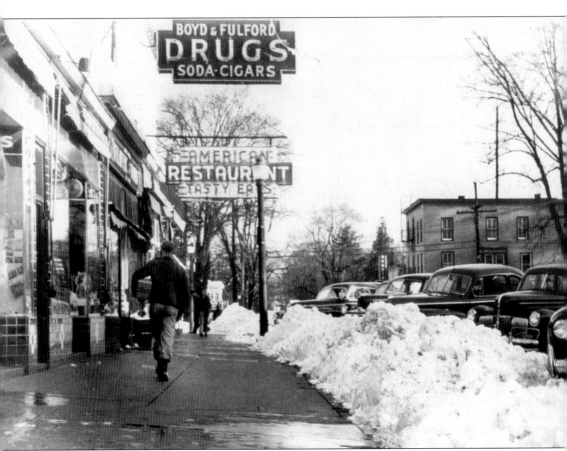

BOYD & FULFORD, SNOWY SIDEWALK, 1958. Although the old drug store has undergone the ravages of the 1972 fire and a 1978 road replacement, its black tile front and the signature B&F entrance steps are still in remarkably fine shape. (Courtesy Gene and Mary Streett, Boyd & Fulford.)

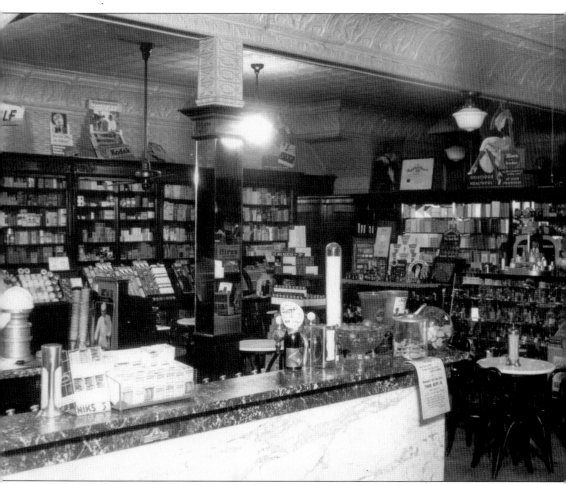

BOYD & FULFORD, INTERIOR, 1934. While a building's exterior can stay the same for decades, an interior changes frequently, if only because of new stock, packaging, and in-store advertising. These wonderful 1934 photos tell the inside story of bygone times through the tin ceiling, rich wood displays, the marble soda fountain, and the products and ads on the soda fountain and cosmetics counter. A 10¢ bottle of Gosman's soda sits on the counter. Atop shelves are ads for Whitman's Candy, Cutex, Kodak, and "deliciously healthful" Hires Root Beer. The flyer on the counter reads: "Notice. Base Ball Game, Chicken Corn Soup Supper, Round Dance at Stambarger's[?] Park, Fawn Grove [Pennsylvania], Thur. Sept. 6." (Courtesy Gene and Mary Streett, Boyd & Fulford.)

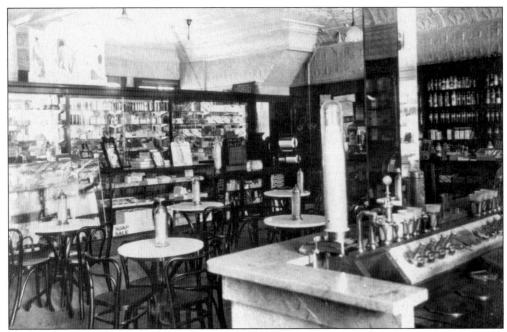

BOYD & FULFORD, INTERIOR, 1934. If you were a Bel Air High student, you would run right to Boyd & Fulford's or Richardson's soda fountain after school. Times change; when a new space-age material called Formica™ came on the market, the Streetts decided to remodel the store. Men came with sledgehammers to break apart the marble and haul it away. (Courtesy Gene and Mary Streett, Boyd & Fulford.)

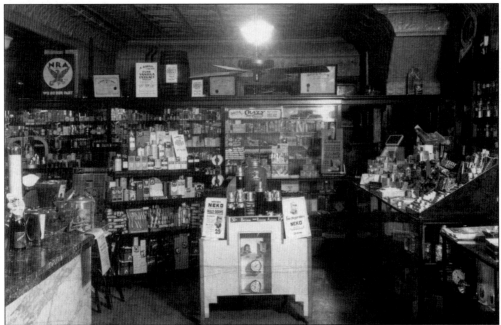

BOYD & FULFORD, INTERIOR, 1934. Products for sale include pure Vanilla Extract $1.39 for 16 oz., Colgate Toothpaste 19¢, Kotex 19¢, and Neko Germicidal Soap ("for chigger bites") 25¢. (Courtesy Gene and Mary Streett, Boyd & Fulford.)

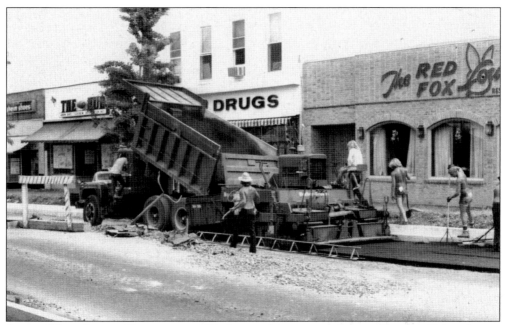

SOUTH MAIN STREET REPAVING, 1978. During the repaving project, Gene and Mary Streett documented the removal of over 900 truckloads of old material and 5,500 tons of new blacktop for the three-block area. Streett noted the female paver operator. (Courtesy Gene and Mary Streett, Boyd & Fulford.)

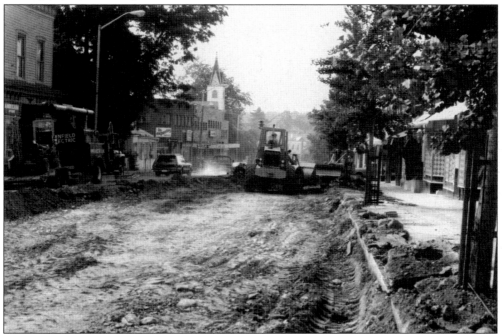

SOUTH MAIN STREET REPAVING, 1978. Looking north from Boyd & Fulford's, Main Street has not had this much dirt on it since horse and buggy days. Water services were upgraded during the project. Immediately after the work was done, the Hub (a clothing store) closed. (Courtesy Gene and Mary Streett, Boyd & Fulford.)

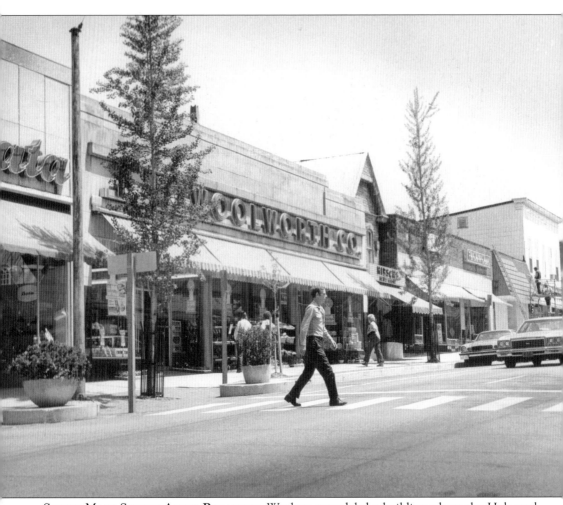

South Main Street After Repaving. Workers remodel the building where the Hub used to be. The familiar peak atop Hirsch's Men's Store is clearly visible. F.W. Woolworth is a familiar sight on Main Streets throughout the nation. The Bata Shoe store is the last building before Pennsylvania Avenue, the street that divides Main Street into South and North. (Courtesy Jim Welsh, Town of Bel Air.)

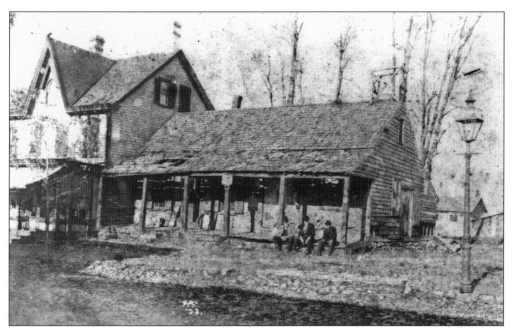

OLD SHOP ON SOUTH MAIN. This undated photo shows the building to the right of what would become Hirsch's Men's Store. See the familiar peak? Fire and feud would not destroy the Hirsch's building over the years, although it has been altered at the sides. This unidentified building, possibly a stable, would transform a number of times over the years. (Courtesy Gene and Mary Streett, Boyd & Fulford.)

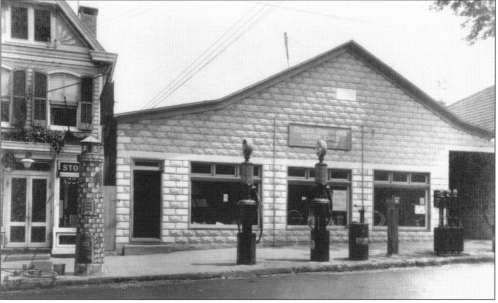

DODGE BROTHERS MOTOR CARS, SOUTH MAIN STREET. Once horse transportation gave way to the motor car, sales and service of the new technology exploded. Car dealerships, garages, and gas stations were everywhere. Main Street was no exception. The charming bus stop lighthouse was painted by George Van Bibber, who lived at the top of South Main. (Courtesy Gene and Mary Streett, Boyd & Fulford.)

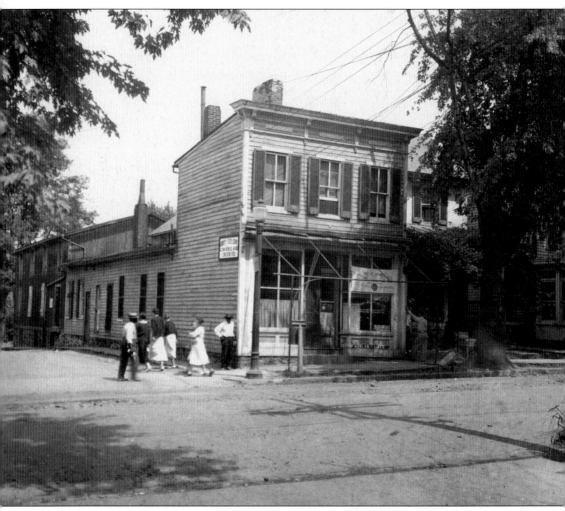

ONE SOUTH MAIN STREET, HARLAN AND LUTZ. The first building on South Main has transformed from Liberty Feed Store (in back in this photo) to Buontempo Bros. Restaurant in 80 years. It has housed a hardware store, Bata Shoes, Frank's Pizza, and, as shown in this *c.* 1929 photo, Charles Lutz's first enterprise, a partnership with Edwin Harlan selling Maytag washers and Norge refrigerators. One of the Maytags sits on the sidewalk to the right of the store, where two men chat or do business. (Courtesy Charles L. Lutz, Inc.)

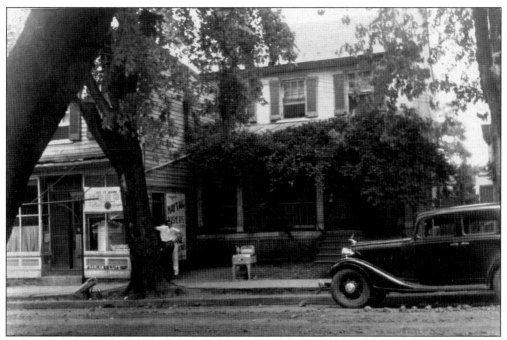

ONE SOUTH MAIN STREET, HARLAN AND LUTZ. Those two guys don't move much, do they? Charles Lutz went on to become one of Bel Air's busiest businessmen, buying, selling, and developing properties all over town, including his own appliance store at 8 North Main Street. (Courtesy Charles L. Lutz, Inc.)

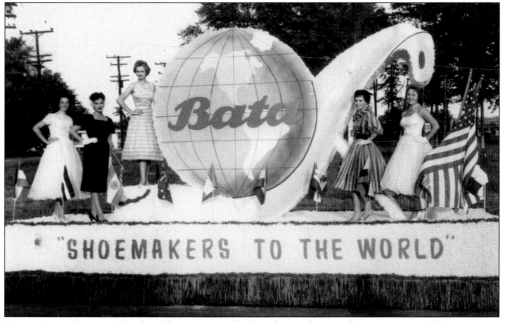

BATA SHOE FLOAT. The headline says it all: from housedress to haute couture. The occasion and date are unidentified, but those ever-present telephone and power lines could indicate a holiday parade in Bel Air. The Bata Shoe factory was located in Belcamp in Harford County. (Courtesy the Historical Society of Harford County, Inc.)

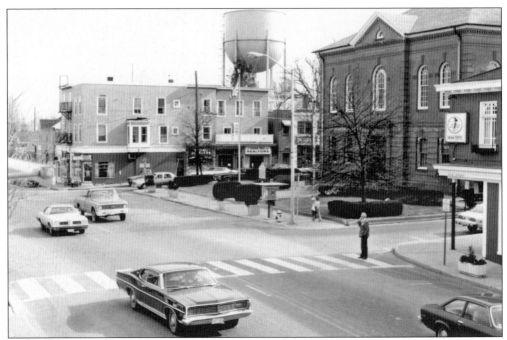

THE COURT HOUSE BEFORE REPAVING, 1978. Back at the south end of South Main and across the street is another landmark, the Stagmer Hotel, just at the corner of Courtland and Main (toward the upper left of the photo). (Courtesy Gene and Mary Streett, Boyd & Fulford.)

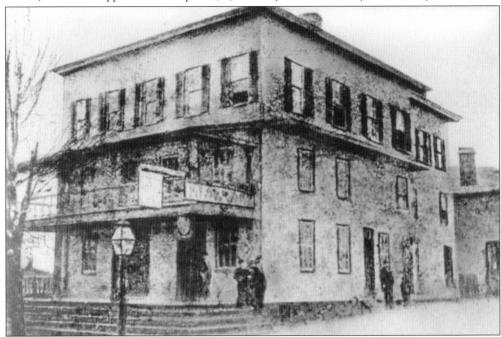

THE STAGMER HOTEL. This image of the Stagmer is from an early postcard. Why so many hotels in such a small town? When travel is slow, as it was with horses, trains, and early autos, people needed places to rest and to get out of bad weather. There were also visitors with legal business to attend to. (Courtesy the Historical Society of Harford County, Inc.)

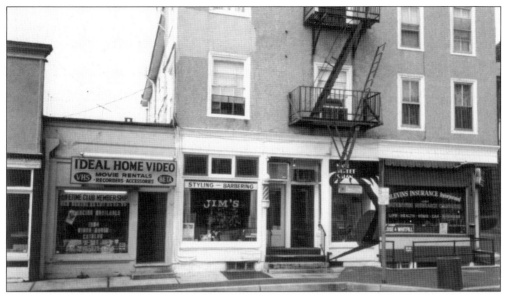

STAGMER HOTEL STOREFRONTS, 1984. One hotel guest in 1932 sent this message home via postcard: "Dear Bobby, We got here about eleven o'clock last night. Daddy is out buying cows. Hope you are all right. Look after business & help Harold & Minnie while we are away. Had the car washed this morning. Love Mother." (Courtesy the Historical Society of Harford County, Inc.)

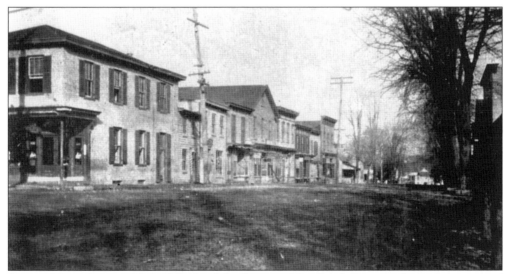

SOUTH MAIN STREET VIEW. North of the Stagmer Hotel and the court house is a group of South Main shops and offices that, like their counterparts across the street, have changed considerably over the years, although some names have remained the same. (Courtesy the Historical Society of Harford County, Inc.)

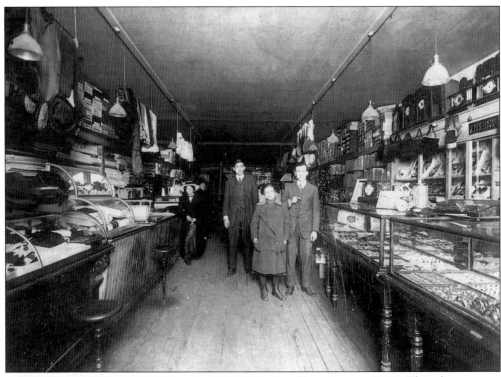

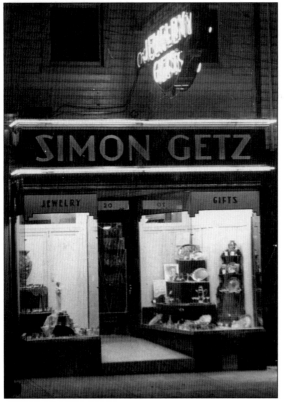

GETZ STORE, 1918. This photo shows the Getz family in 1918 when Solomon ran the business. Later, sons David and Simon took over and featured their specialties of clothing, optometry, and jewelry. The brothers would soon run separate shops: Getz Clothing Store and Getz Jewelry Store, the first location. Pictured are, from left to right, the following: Louis Getz, Hattie Getz, and Simon Getz. (Courtesy Payson Getz.)

SIMON GETZ STORE, 1936. Simon Getz remodeled 20 South Main Street according to the Art Deco fashion of the times. His jewelry and gift shop was passed down to his son, Payson, who continued it, moved it to North Main Street for a while, and then moved to the new Harford Mall in 1972. Then he moved back to South Main and sold the business to the Johnston brothers. New generations of Getzes running their own businesses keep the family name present on Main Street. (Courtesy Payson Getz.)

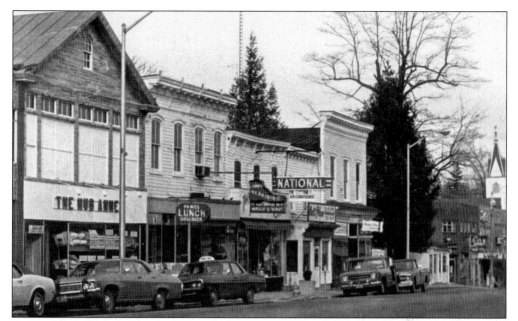

SOUTH MAIN STREET VIEW. Although the sign at 22 South Main has the words Lunch Panos Grill Beer, Mrs. Panos's place was known as the Candy Kitchen and is still remembered as such by many in Bel Air. George Van Bibber was a regular, going there every afternoon for a soda. (Courtesy the Historical Society of Harford County, Inc.)

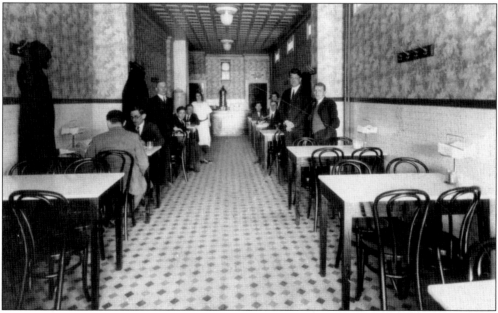

THE CANDY KITCHEN. A recent remodeling of 22 South Main for the new De Danann Coffee and Tea Shop revealed several layers of subflooring and at least four different colors of paint layered on the walls. The original Candy Kitchen tin ceiling, visible in this photo, lies underneath a false ceiling. Dave Cohen of Hirsch's Men's Store thinks this photo was taken soon after Mrs. Panos's arrival in Bel Air in 1914. (Courtesy the Historical Society of Harford County, Inc.)

47

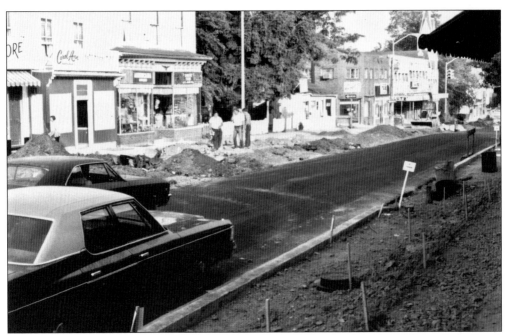

SOUTH MAIN STREET REPAVING, 1978. This is a later view of the stretch of shops along South Main. All of these buildings have been razed for new brick buildings in a more or less Colonial style. The small white building at the end of South Main was the Fulton Harness Shop, which dated back to 1850. (Courtesy Gene and Mary Streett, Boyd & Fulford.)

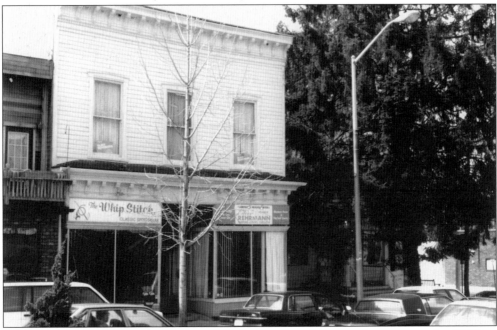

THE WHIP STITCH. This building housed the Bel Air Post Office until its move to the Old Post Office building at Main and Gordon Streets. The new Bel Air Post Office sits behind the Harford Mall complex, just within town limits. (Courtesy the Historical Society of Harford County, Inc.)

Three

ALONG NORTH MAIN STREET

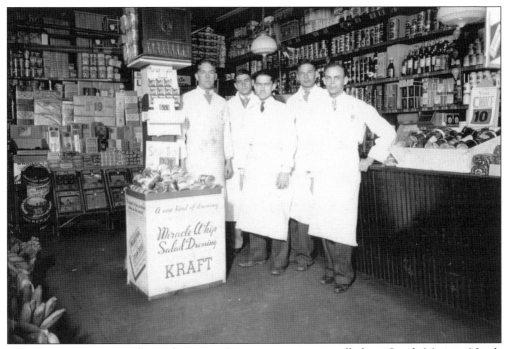

THE AMERICAN STORE (ACME), 1933. As we move on our walk from South Main to North Main, consider the Acme food store in its first location on Courtland Street. We will see it again later on North Main. Pictured are, from left to right, the following: Denwood Bowman, butcher; Edward Robinson; John Bedford; John Guggenheim; and Hillman Levinson, merchant. (Courtesy the Historical Society of Harford County, Inc.)

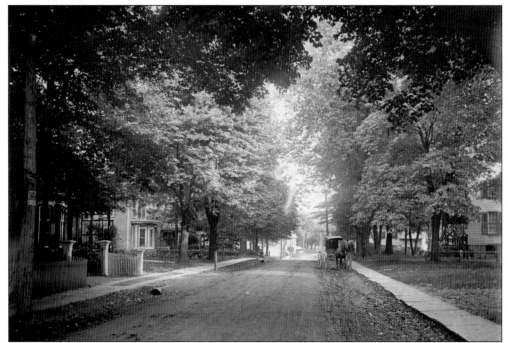

NORTH MAIN STREET VIEW. This is another original photo from which the postcard was created. The Hopkins House is second on the left. The sidewalks are slate slabs from nearby Delta, Pennsylvania. The road is dirt with an early pipe sewer system. The hitching posts outside each home indicate that autos had not yet made inroads (literally) into Bel Air at this time. (Courtesy Gene and Mary Streett, Boyd & Fulford.)

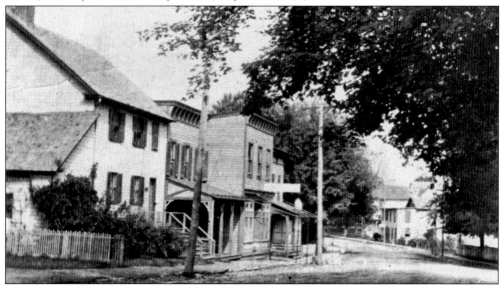

NORTH MAIN STREET VIEW. At the leftmost stands the Graham-Crocker House, today used as offices. It was built on the very first of those 42 half-acre lots on Scott's Old Fields. The original owner must not have liked the cold Bel Air winters: the walls are insulated with red cedar shavings and each room has a fireplace. (Courtesy the Historical Society of Harford County, Inc.)

50

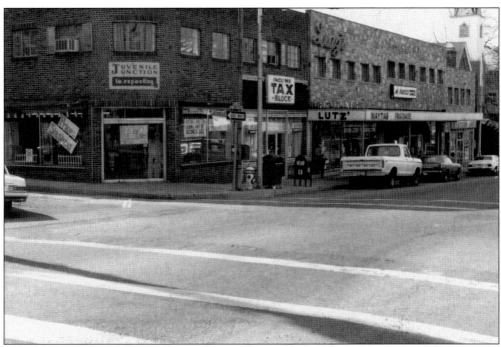

LUTZ BUILDING, 1978. The northeast corner of Main Street and Pennsylvania Avenue was bought and cleared by Charles Lutz. He developed the property in stages, starting with his appliance store in 1947, and later added a second story and adjacent buildings. The Pennsylvania Avenue side goes back to Bond Street, where Fritz and Peggy Kelly ran a laundry service. (Courtesy Gene and Mary Streett, Boyd & Fulford.)

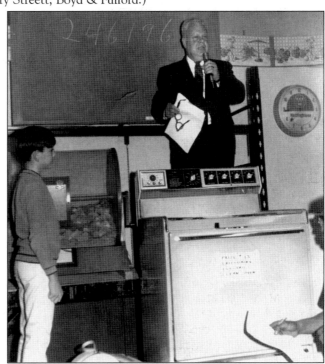

LUTZ HOLIDAY PRIZE DRAWING. For many years at Lutz's, each customer was given a ticket with the purchase of an appliance. On a special day before Christmas, people packed the store to watch as Charles Lutz drew ticket numbers and awarded free prizes like the Frigidaire electric clean oven in the photo. Note the hopper of tickets to the left. (Courtesy Charles L. Lutz, Inc.)

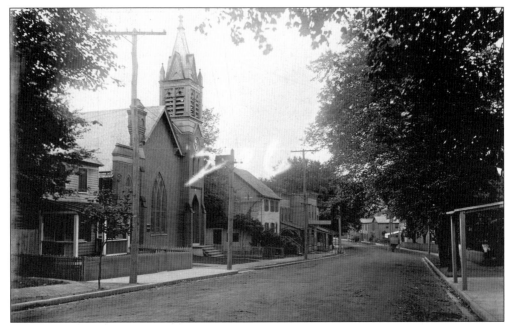

METHODIST EPISCOPAL CHURCH. Built in 1888 for $8,000 and used until the new church was built in 1968, the church was the Harford Center and has now been remodeled as offices for county non-profit agencies. Divisions, reorganizations, and expansions of the Methodist congregations over the years account for the number of Methodist church buildings in the area. (Courtesy Gene and Mary Streett, Boyd & Fulford.)

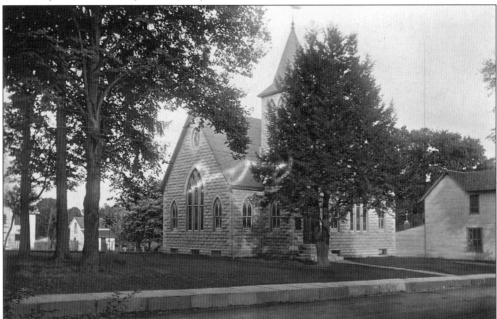

GRACE METHODIST PROTESTANT CHURCH. Shown in another postcard proof photo, the original 1884 church burned and was rebuilt in 1908. Used as a church until 1943, it was later one of the many borrowed locations for the public library. The church was near the southeast corner of North Main and Lee Streets. (Courtesy Gene and Mary Streett, Boyd & Fulford.)

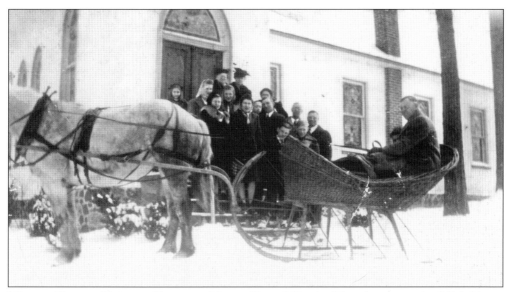

MOUNT CARMEL BAPTIST CHURCH. Mount Carmel Baptist Church was north of Bel Air on Route 22. This c. 1930 photo shows members of the Edwards family and others. Pictured are, from left to right, the following: unidentified man in sleigh; (first row) unidentified and Charles Edwards; (second row) unidentified, Clyde Choate, Thomas Weaver, Rev. ? Thompson, and Thomas Edwards; (third row) unidentified, Hazel Moxley, Lois Edwards (Nagle), and two unidentified; (fourth row) Mrs. Maude Thompson and Pearl Edwards.

METHODIST EPISCOPAL CHURCH. A post-1968 photo of the church reveals its repurposed use as a polyglot center: a sign on the door identifies the site as the Bel Air Youth Center, while a sign for the Department of Inspections, Licensing, and Permits indicates county use of the facility as well. (Courtesy the Historical Society of Harford County, Inc.)

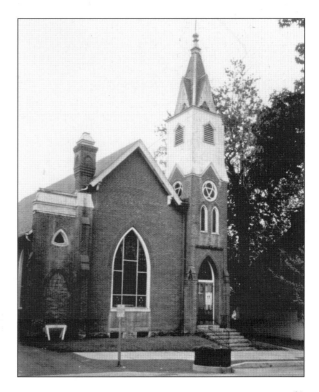

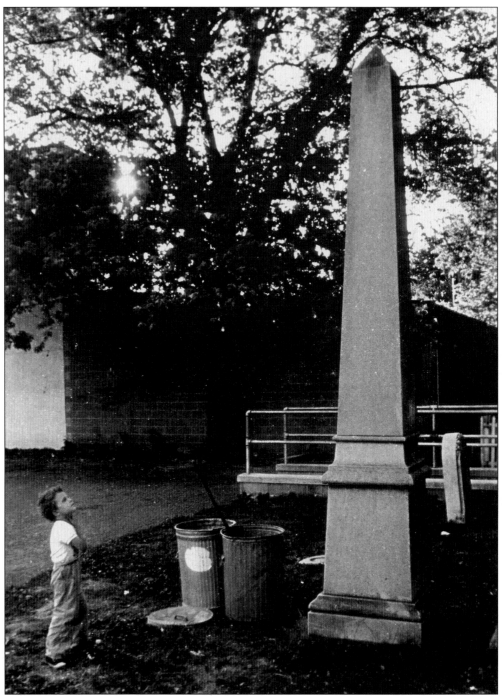

METHODIST EPISCOPAL CHURCH CEMETERY. When the space behind the church was scheduled for development, something had to be done with the graveyard. This Wayde Chrismer photo seems to ask eternal questions as workers prepared to move remains and monuments, which were relocated to Emmorton. (Courtesy the Historical Society of Harford County, Inc.)

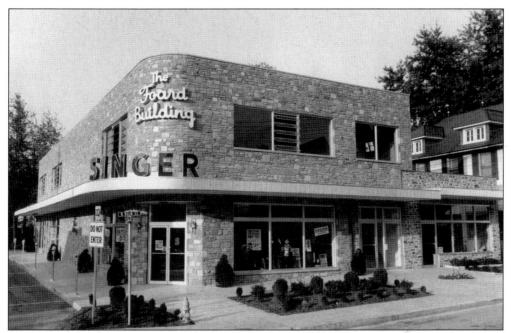

THE FOARD BUILDING. In 1967, Charles Lutz bought the property at North Main and Lee Streets, which included an apartment building. He tore this down to build the first part of what became the Foard Building. Like the property on North Main and Pennsylvania, the Foard Building was created in stages, as seen in these two photos. (Courtesy Charles L. Lutz, Inc.)

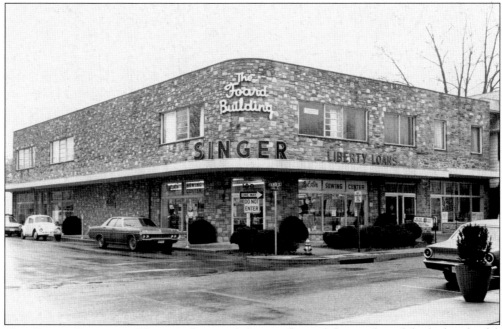

THE FOARD BUILDING. The completion of the top floor of the north end (right-hand side) brought unity to the mix of storefronts and office spaces. Like its counterpart up the street, the building goes back and around to Bond Street, where Fisher Auto Parts leases space. (Courtesy Charles L. Lutz, Inc.)

55

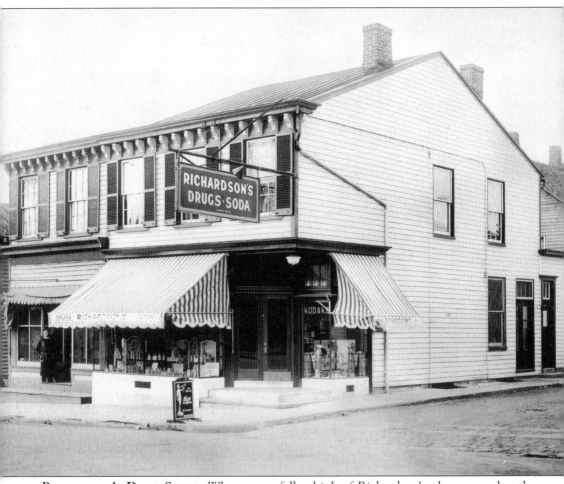

RICHARDSON'S DRUG STORE. When many folks think of Richardson's, they remember the soda fountain and chocolate milkshakes like no others on earth, the cherry cokes, or the vanilla cokes: a tall glass of soda water, a shot of coke syrup, a pull of real vanilla syrup from the gleaming steel pump, and a paper straw. The sidewalk sign proclaims: "We serve Horn's Ice Cream. It's quality. Baltimore's Best!" Displays in the shop windows advertise cold cream, vanishing cream, and Kodak film. John Richardson began his drug store on the southwest corner of North Main Street and Pennsylvania Avenue in the early 1900s. George Van Bibber recalled a dentist, Dr. Warren, and the Bel Air Library in rooms on the second floor of the drug store. You will see how the shop would continue to change and grow over the years; this and the next seven photos trace that progression. (Courtesy the Historical Society of Harford County, Inc.)

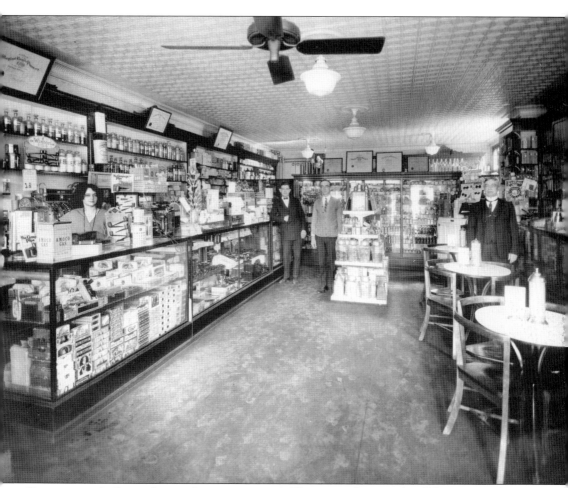

RICHARDSON'S DRUG STORE, INTERIOR, 1925. This atmospheric and well-lit interior photo of the drug store shows what it was like to live in a place where Main Street was unpaved. Dusty footprints cover the floor, and the men's shoes are covered with dust. The dirty condition must have been unremarkable, or certainly the men would have cleaned up for the photographer. Note the tin ceiling, ceiling lights, and fan. Cigars and pipes fill the left counters, and gift items and jars of penny candy are stocked on the display in the middle of the floor. Three small lunch tables hug the right side of the store. (Courtesy the Historical Society of Harford County, Inc.)

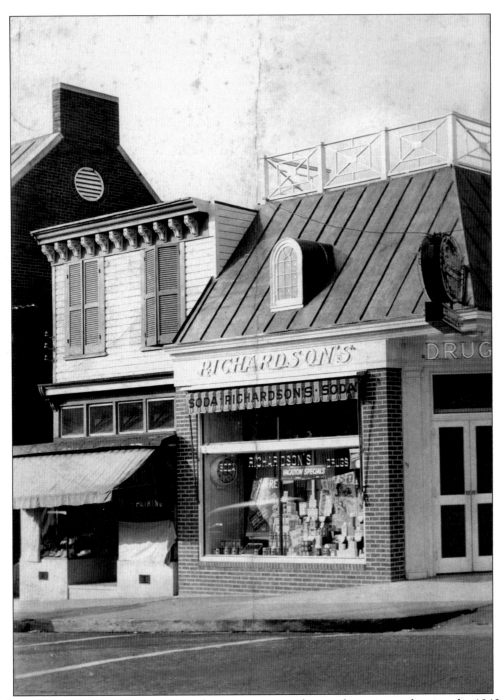

RICHARDSON'S DRUG STORE. This photo is a section of a very large image showing the 1940 remodeling of the drug store. The brick side of the Argonne Theater two doors down is visible. The Bel Air Shoe Repairing Shop is still to the left of the drug store. Gone from Richardson's is the awning that hid both the sun and the window contents from view. New windows let passersby see what's available or on special, ushering in a new era of the impulse buy. (Courtesy the Historical Society of Harford County, Inc.)

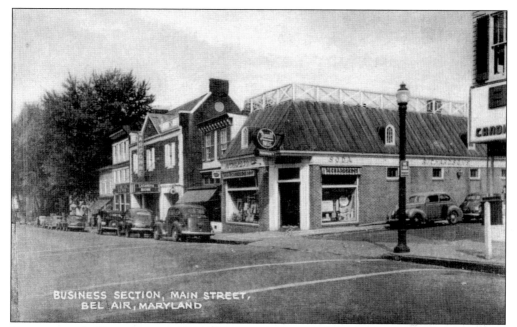

RICHARDSON'S DRUG STORE, 1944. "This pictures one of our drug stores and movies and a little of Main Street." This terse note, written on the back of this unsent postcard (presumably by Phyllis Larch, whose name is also on the back), describes the top-of-mind features of Main Street: the movies and drug store. The other shops are unremarkable for the most part. What most people recall vividly is the entertainment: the movies, the lunch counters, the hangouts of every era. *Casanova Brown*, playing at the Argonne, starred Gary Cooper, Teresa Wright, Frank Morgan, and Anita Louise in a risqué sex comedy. (Courtesy the Historical Society of Harford County, Inc.)

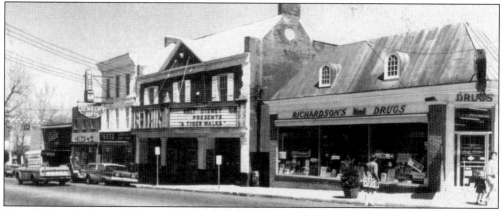

RICHARDSON'S DRUG STORE, 1964. Upon the death of Lloyd Richardson, John Deems bought the drug store. The shoe shop was incorporated into the drug store in 1957, effectively doubling its width front to back. The Argonne has changed hands and is now the Bel Air Movie Theater. Simon Getz's wife, Kate, and their son, Payson, took over the jewelry and gift business and moved it next to the Bel Air Theater in 1954. The original Argonne building has become Reiser's Economy Store. The Kiddie Shop rounds out the 1964 block of stores. (Courtesy the Historical Society of Harford County, Inc.)

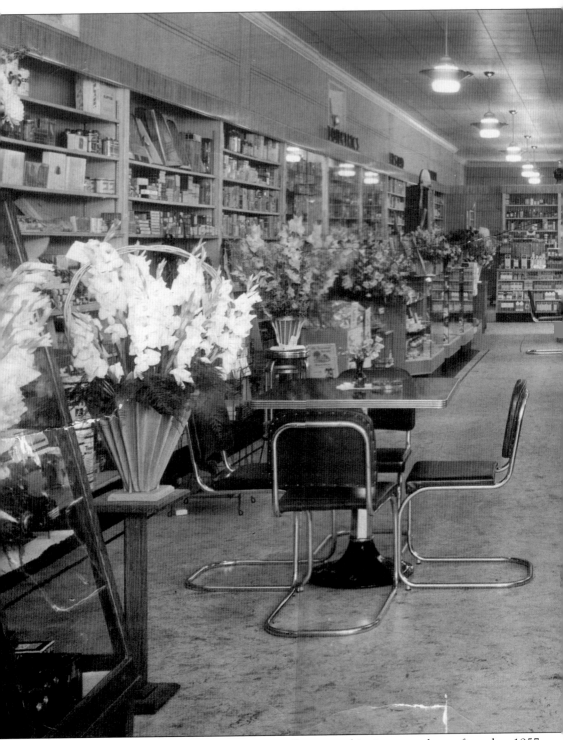

RICHARDSON'S DRUG STORE, INTERIOR. Contrast this image, taken after the 1957 remodeling, with the 1925 photo on page 57. The store is bigger, brighter, and more beautiful.

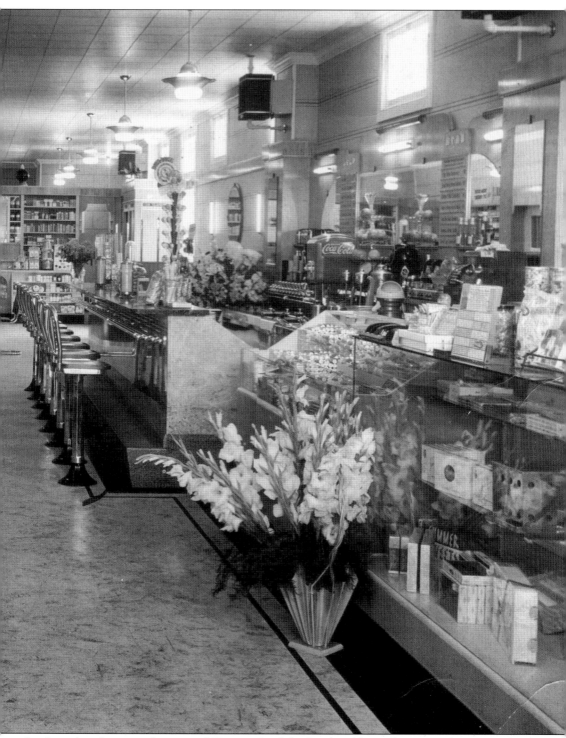

Look at the gleaming chrome and Formica® of the lunch tables and counter. (Courtesy the Historical Society of Harford County, Inc.)

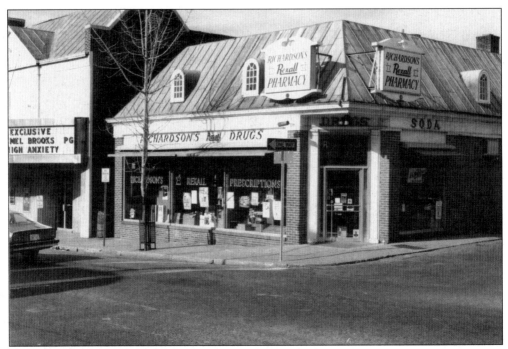

RICHARDSON'S DRUG STORE, 1978. This photo was taken just before the 1978 repaving of Main Street. The Bel Air Theater is showing *High Anxiety*, a Hitchcock spoof by Mel Brooks. The repaving seemed to be a spur for a number of older buildings to be torn down or remodeled, and it coincided with the end of some of downtown's signature businesses, such as the Hub. (Courtesy Gene and Mary Streett, Boyd & Fulford.)

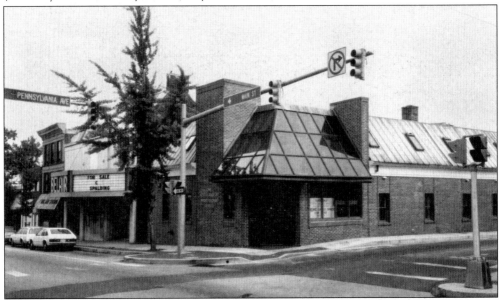

ONE NORTH MAIN STREET. Richardson's has been remodeled into office space, which was just being leased when this photo was taken. The Bel Air Theater is also on the block. More about the transformation of the theater building follows. (Courtesy the Historical Society of Harford County, Inc.)

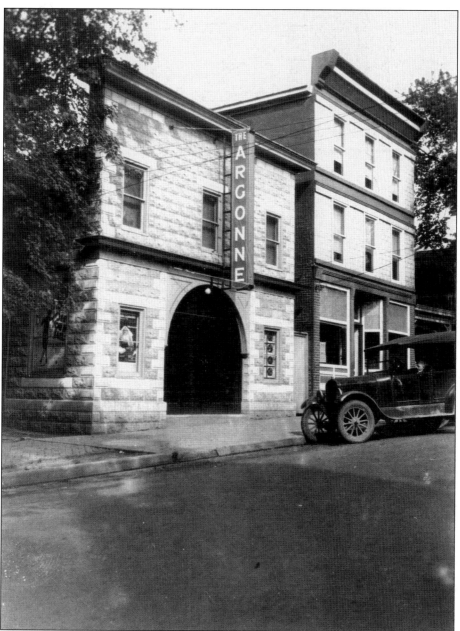

THE ORIGINAL ARGONNE MOVIE THEATER, 1927. The poster in the side window advertises the movie *See You In Jail*, a comedy starring Jack Mulhall, Alice Day, and Mack Swain. George Van Bibber recalled the original Argonne, named for the World War I battle in which the theater's owner had taken part. To provide music for the silent films, the Argonne had a pianola, a piano that one could play manually as a regular piano, or that would play by itself when a roll of music was inserted into the mechanism. Without regard for the mood of the movie's scene, the owner's wife would insert any kind of music just to keep the sound going. Sometimes a slow hymn tune might accompany an exciting chase scene. By 1929, the owners had built the new Argonne Theater, two doors south on North Main Street. (Courtesy Charles L. Lutz, Inc.)

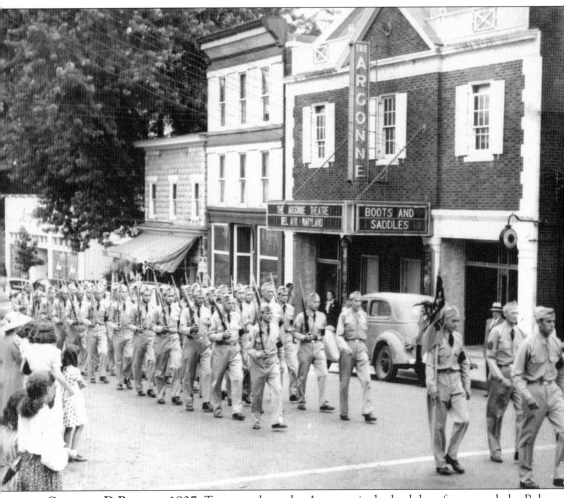

COMPANY D PARADE, 1937. Ten years later the Argonne is the backdrop for a parade by Bel Air's own Maryland Guard Unit Company D. The new theater is larger, with more seating and a balcony, and features an organ larger than any church organ in town. Of course, talkies are established and musicals are all the rage, as are westerns. On the marquee is *Boots and Saddles*, an action-filled, romantic western musical adventure starring Gene Autry, Smiley Burnette, and Judith Allen. Our buildings mark our pride as well as our scars: Jim Welsh recalls that part of the balcony had been set aside for blacks during the years of segregation. Next to the theatre is Dean and Foster, originally a furniture and funeral provider (wood furniture, wood caskets, etc). The original Argonne has become Reiser's Economy Store, and the Acme food store is north of that. (Courtesy the Historical Society of Harford County, Inc.)

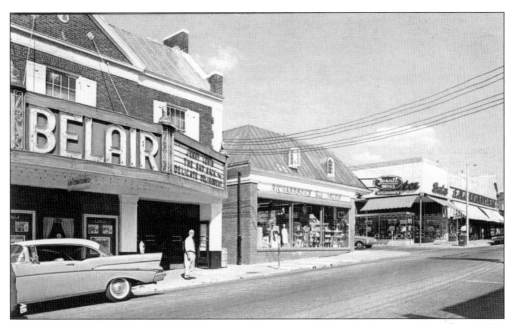

BEL AIR MOVIE THEATER, 1957. The postcard images on this page show two views from 1957. The top picture shows Richardson's Drug Store after the remodeling that incorporated the old shoe store, which, by the time of the remodeling (see bottom photo), had become Lilo's Art Gallery. Two Jerry Lewis movies in one year? Adam Sandler should have it so good. (Courtesy the Historical Society of Harford County, Inc.)

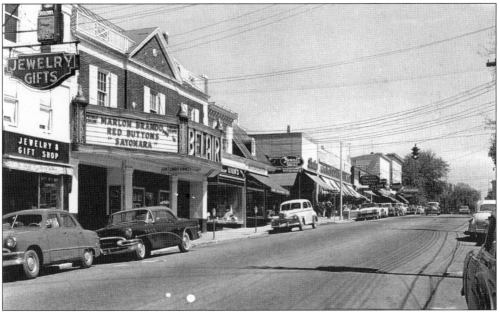

BEL AIR MOVIE THEATER, 1957. Robin Sommer recalls special Saturdays when she and her high school classmates were offered discount movie prices to sit in the balcony to help fill the house. The theater still had a good 20 years to go as bel Air's neighborhood movie house. Years later, the original Argonne was given a new brick façade over the original block. (Courtesy Marcus Johnston.)

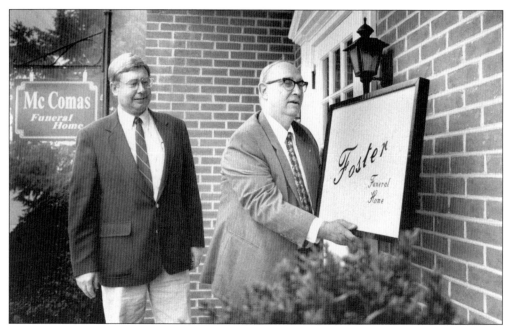

FOSTER FUNERAL HOME, 1994. The Dean and Foster furniture/funeral partnership lasted on North Main Street until Edward Dean died in 1945. Then Joseph Foster built a funeral home a few blocks away on Broadway and Williams Street. Here Joe Foster Jr. removes his sign as Howard McComas, the new owner, prepares to take over the business. (Courtesy *The Aegis*.)

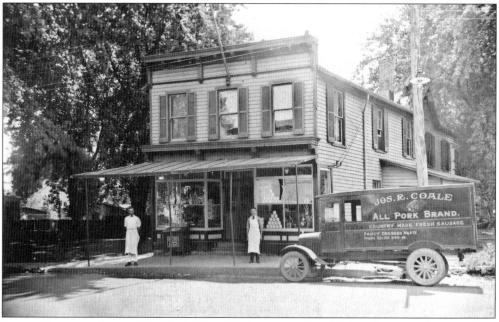

JOSEPH R. COALE STORE. The Coale Meat Market was on South Main Street on the site where the Vaughn Hotel would be built. It was in business from the late 1800s until the mid-1920s. His son ran a food store on North Main Street. Contrast Coale's and the American Store (Acme) pictured on page 49 with the new self-serve supermarkets. (Courtesy the Historical Society of Harford County, Inc.)

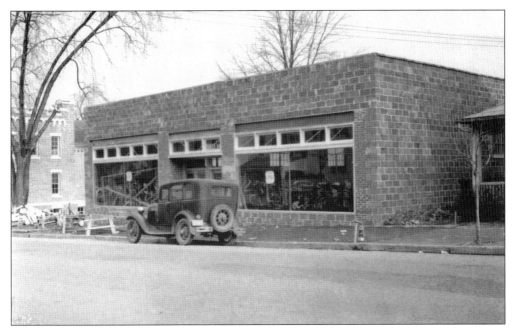

ACME FOOD STORE, 1942. Once the property of a Mr. Whittaker, whose attractive frame house and nice side yard were admired by George Van Bibber, the new, low Acme Food Store represented a different kind of store. The building's design was part of the train garden town of Plasticville, but in truth the new supermarket made no attempt to fit into the architecture of small-town America. (Courtesy Craig Ward.)

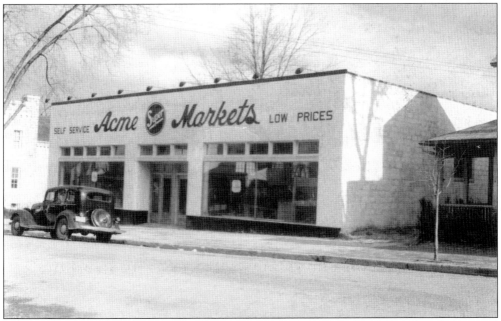

ACME FOOD STORE, 1942. The new Acme food store represented a new philosophy in retail food sales: self-service. Instead of having a clerk put your food order together for you, you could get lower prices by doing the job of collecting your order yourself and taking it to a cashier. (Courtesy Craig Ward.)

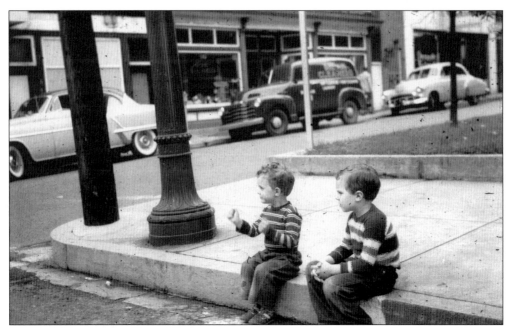

NORTH MAIN STREET VIEW. The Acme outgrew its North Main Street building and became the anchor store at the new Fallston Mall at Routes 1 and 152. Main Street begins a slow transformation as stores such as the Acme, A&P, and Woolworth's move away from Main Street to the new shopping centers. Once-busy storefronts threaten to sit empty. (Courtesy the Historical Society of Harford County, Inc.)

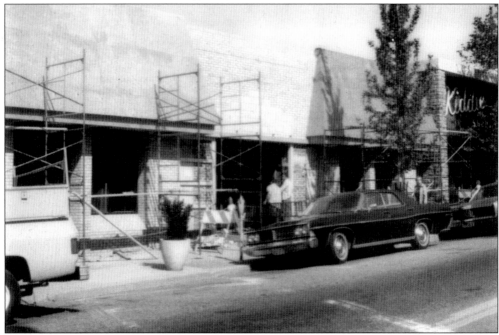

23 NORTH MAIN STREET. After the Acme store moved, Beshore's, a mom and pop furniture store, inhabited the building. This photo is from the 1980s, when Frederick Ward Associates redesigned and modernized the former food store building for offices. (Courtesy Craig Ward.)

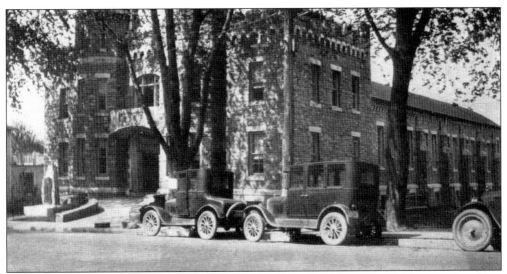

BEL AIR ARMORY. On his way to a swimming hole, little George Van Bibber would stop to watch the progress of the construction of the armory. There was a long period of inactivity due to funding problems, but by 1915 Van Bibber finally "saw these steel trusses being put into place and the big arch roof and it was fascinating to watch." (Courtesy the Historical Society of Harford County, Inc.)

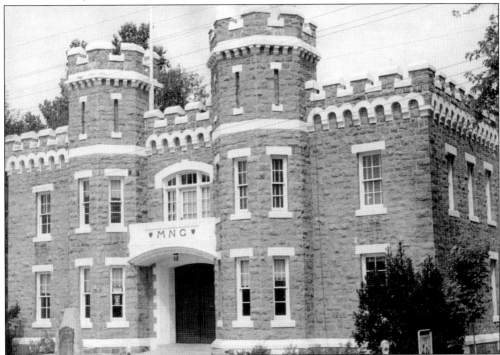

BEL AIR ARMORY. What took place at the armory? George Van Bibber recalled: "Drilling for Company D and later on another outfit, but also high school graduations were held here and the famous armory dances, dances for the DAR, dances for the Red Cross, dances for the library, dances for Company D, and all sorts of affairs were held here." (Courtesy the Historical Society of Harford County, Inc.)

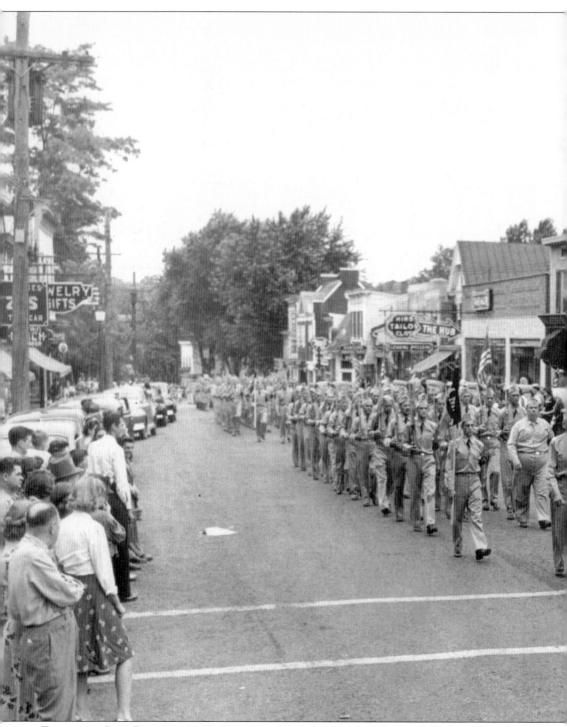

FOURTH OF JULY PARADE, 1943. Company D marches up Main Street. Folks line Main Street from the Vaughn Hotel (note the people on the balcony), to the American Restaurant (later the Red Fox), the Hub, Boyd & Fulford's Drug Store, Hirsch's with its distinctive peaked roof, all the way down to the Argonne Theater and its familiar roofline. Company D had a long

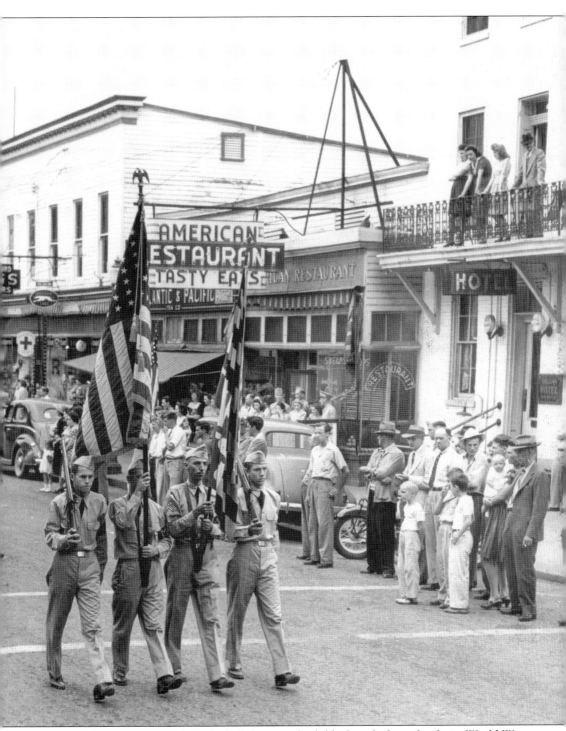

history as a heavy armament brigade. Bel Air men, both black and white, fought in World War I (in Argonne) and World War II (on Omaha Beach on D-Day), and in the Spanish-American War. In the 1960s Company D became an attack helicopter unit. (Courtesy the Historical Society of Harford County, Inc.)

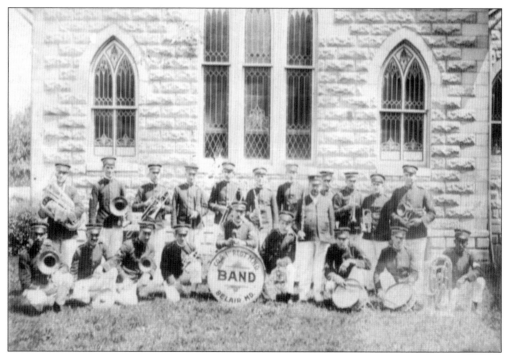

COMPANY D BAND, 1925. Grouped in front of Grace Methodist Protestant Church, the men of Company D of the 1st Regiment Infantry of the Maryland National Guard Band pose for a photo. (Courtesy the Historical Society of Harford County, Inc.)

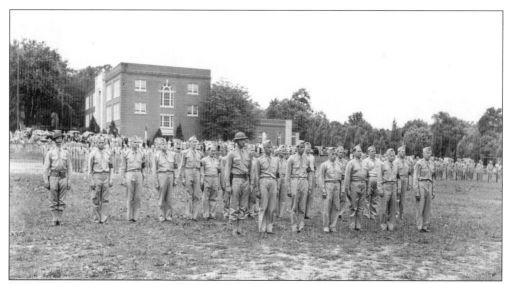

FOURTH OF JULY PARADE, 1943. Company D gathers in formation and prepares for the march onto Main Street for the annual parade. The old Bel Air High School is visible in the background. (Courtesy the Historical Society of Harford County, Inc.)

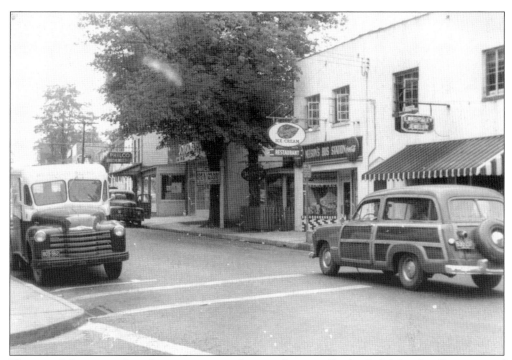

VIEW OF MAIN AND LEE STREETS, 1949. Payson Getz recalls the Bel–Mar Cut Rate, one of the first discount stores. The store attempted to attract customers and do serious damage to establishments such as Richardson's by shaving pennies off the prices of over-the-counter medicines. Note the Mt. Ararat Farms truck on the left, delivering dairy products to homes throughout Bel Air. (Courtesy the Historical Society of Harford County, Inc.)

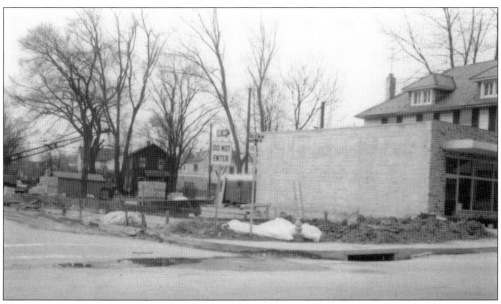

VIEW OF MAIN AND LEE STREETS, 1967. On the northwest side of Main and Lee, the Foard Building is just taking shape. (Courtesy the Historical Society of Harford County, Inc.)

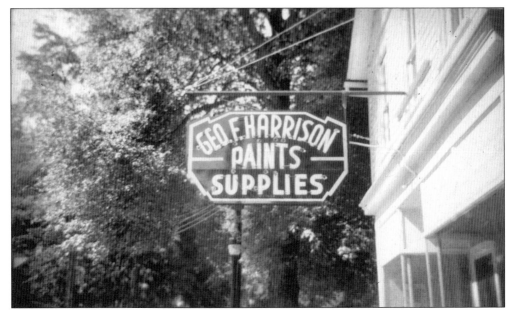

HARRISON'S PAINT SUPPLIES SIGN. George Harrison's sign was typical of the neon signs that Maryland regulated out of existence in the 1960s as a beautification and safety measure. In many areas, businesses cluttered the streets with bigger, brighter, and busier signs. The signs were also hung dangerously far out from their buildings for added visibility. Now neon is making a comeback. (Courtesy the Historical Society of Harford County, Inc.)

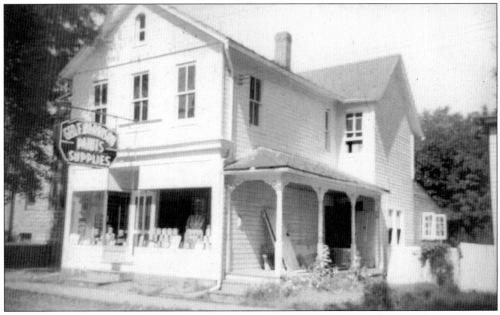

HARRISON'S PAINT SUPPLIES. The original store was the Harrison home with the paint store at the street level. As was typical of many of Bel Air's shopkeepers, the Harrisons lived upstairs from their store. The building is an antique shop in 2004. (Courtesy the Historical Society of Harford County, Inc.)

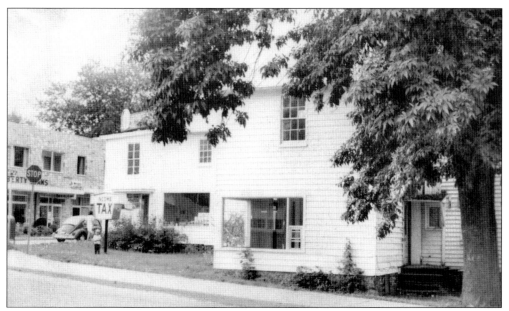

BUILDING AT MAIN AND LEE STREETS, 1969. When George Harrison needed to expand his store, he tore down this building, which was being used as offices for a tax service, at North Main and Lee Streets. He built Harrison's Paint Center on the corner with the prominent giant paint can on the front. In early 2004 George Jr. sold the business to Rick and Stephanie Daley, Harford County natives. (Courtesy George Harrison Jr.)

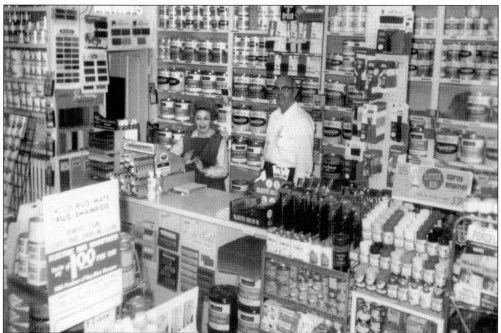

HARRISON'S PAINT SUPPLIES, 1969. Pictured are Helen Harrison and employee Harold Lloyd. Under George Jr., the new store stocked a large supply of home decorating supplies for the indoors and outdoors, including a vast selection of wallpapers, deck staining and cleaning products, and wall finishes for faux and special painting effects. (Courtesy George Harrison Jr.)

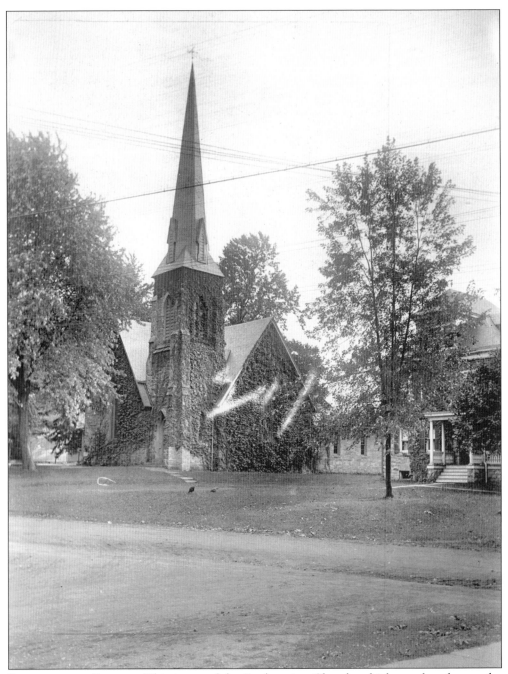

PRESBYTERIAN CHURCH. This image of the Presbyterian Church, which stands today on the southwest corner of Broadway and North Main Street, is a proof photo from the same postcard series as the image on the opposite page, which was taken in August 1923 of Emmanuel Episcopal Church. Many of the previous postcard images were photographed in the winter, which kept the buildings from being obscured by Bel Air's trees. However, notice in these church photos how the greenery adds to the feeling of life, to the sense of a place set apart for contemplation. (Courtesy Gene and Mary Streett, Boyd & Fulford.)

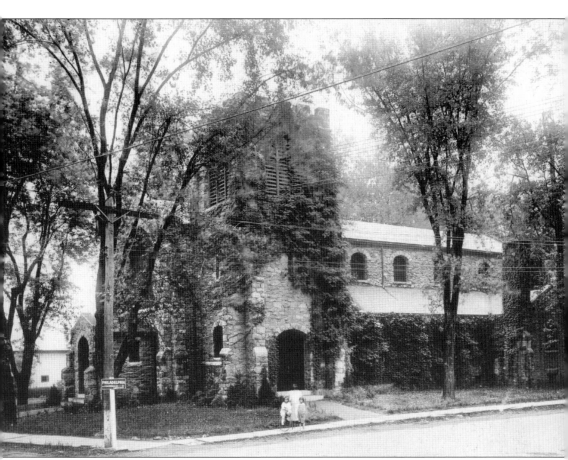

EMMANUEL EPISCOPAL CHURCH, 1923. Maryterese Streett identifies the people in the photo as probably McComas children and a nanny. Note a carryover from the Victorian era: the ivy was allowed to cover the outside of the building. For more on Bel Air churches past and present, visit www.belairbook.com. (Courtesy Gene and Mary Streett, Boyd & Fulford.)

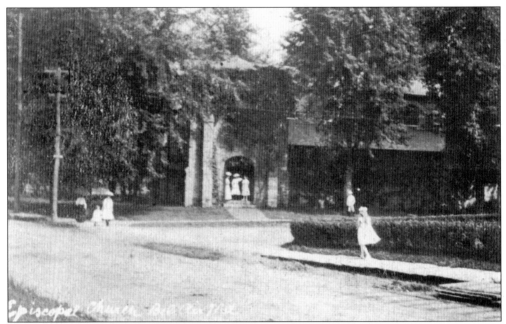

EMMANUEL EPISCOPAL CHURCH. Members of the McComas family are seen again in this postcard image of the church. Note that in this earlier, undated postcard the tower has not yet been finished. (Courtesy the Historical Society of Harford County, Inc.)

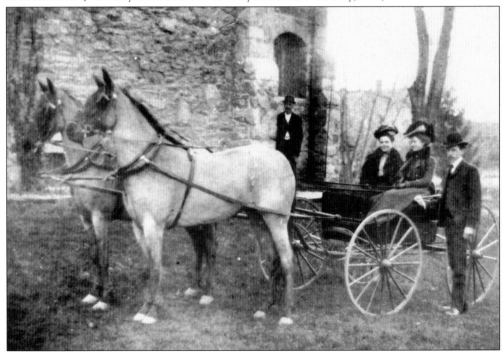

THE McCOMAS FAMILY ARRIVES AT CHURCH, 1912. This photo takes us back to our earliest images in this book, showing vividly the method of getting the family to church, and most everywhere else, from Bel Air's first days well into the early 1900s. Note the formal clothing suitable for the cooler weather. (Courtesy Gene and Mary Streett, Boyd & Fulford.)

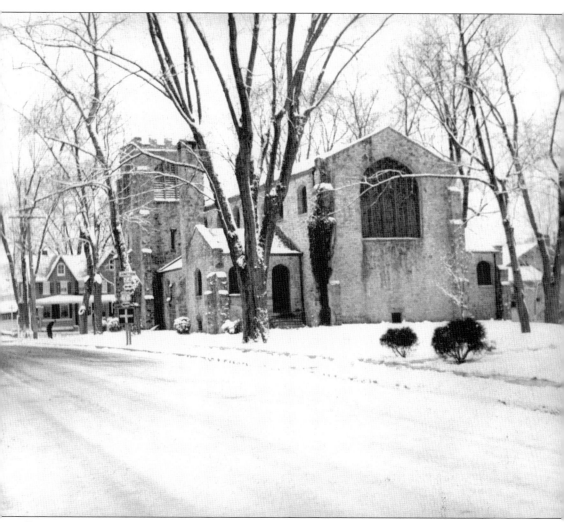

EMMANUEL EPISCOPAL CHURCH, WINTER. Designed by the same architects who created nearby Liriodendron Mansion, the stone church looks beautiful in light of all seasons. Here, even in the frost of a winter snow, the church exudes a warm grandeur that gives it the aura of a medieval cathedral. (Courtesy the Historical Society of Harford County, Inc.)

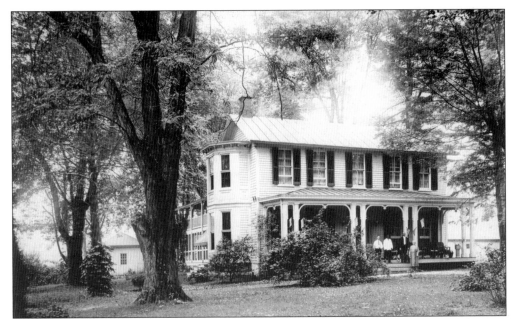

YEW TREE INN, 1923. Once located on the northwest corner of Gordon and North Main Streets, the Yew Tree Inn was converted to an inn from a home built in the early 1800s. The inn was torn down in 1950 for the new headquarters of the Harford Mutual Insurance Company, which had outgrown its Office Street building. Note the formality of dress, despite the August heat. (Courtesy Gene and Mary Streett, Boyd & Fulford.)

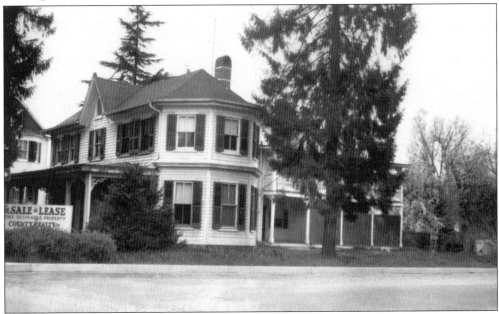

THE CIRCLE INN. Another home of the 1800s, the Circle Inn was converted to a boarding house in 1919 by a Mrs. Forwood. It stood on the northeast corner of Gordon and Main Streets. Maryterese Streett identified Nathan Corbin's house on the left. Klein's Bel Air grocery store and a K Bank branch occupy the space in 2004. (Courtesy the Historical Society of Harford County, Inc.)

Four
THE BOND STREET
AREA

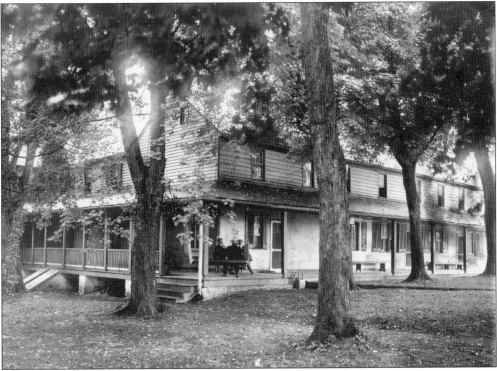

THE EAGLE HOTEL. Not just another Bel Air hotel, the Eagle Hotel, later known as the Country Club Inn, was a resort hotel away from the bustle of Main Street—well, one block away at least. The Eagle flourished from the 1700s to the 1940s. *The Aegis* newspaper of January 5, 1915, reads: "Old Hostler Dies. Ned Taylor, probably the most widely known colored man in Harford County, succumbed on Sunday to the ills incident to old age at his home in Belair [*sic*]. Ned was chief Hostler at the Eagle Hotel for upward of sixty years until it closed, and in its balmy days when there would sometimes be thirty teams fed there at the same time. Ned would never get horses and vehicles interchanged. He was faithful to his employer, honest, polite with everyone, and barring a few shortcomings of the flesh, was a man of many excellent qualities." (Courtesy the Historical Society of Harford County, Inc.)

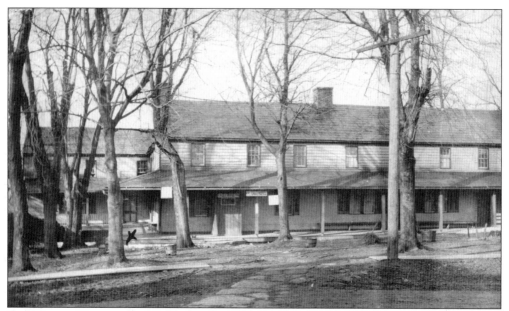

THE EAGLE HOTEL. Some of these photos are from a scrapbook of photos donated to the historical society by the Havre de Grace architect James Thomas Wollon Jr. Handwritten notes from the scrapbook follow: "The old Eagle Hotel now the Country Club Inn at Bel Air. The first part of this building was a log structure built in 1718." As Scott's Old Fields were not developed until the 1780s, the above-noted date of 1718 is unlikely. (Courtesy the Historical Society of Harford County, Inc.)

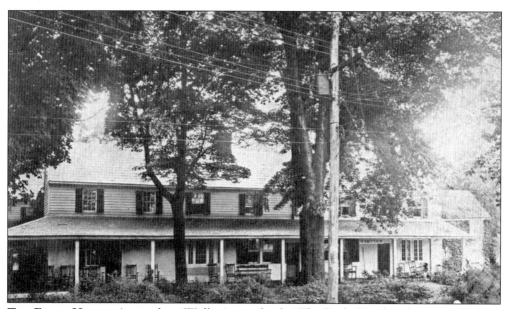

THE EAGLE HOTEL. Again, from Wollen's scrapbook: "The Eagle Hotel, Bel Air, in 1914 . . . was a fashionable hostelry, famous for its fine foods and hospitality. It was torn down in the forties to make way for Bel Air's first shopping center, now occupied by the C-Mart, but recently bought by the County as part of its expansion program." (Courtesy the Historical Society of Harford County, Inc.)

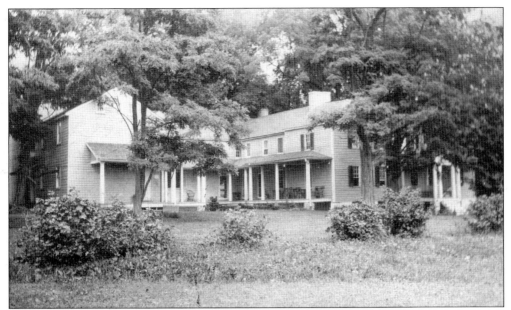

THE EAGLE HOTEL, REAR. Wollen's scrapbook identifies this as "the rear of the 'Eagle Hotel' 1912." This is a rare photo of the back porch sitting area with a small planted area with mini shrubs. The postcards and other typical views show the front only. (Courtesy the Historical Society of Harford County, Inc.)

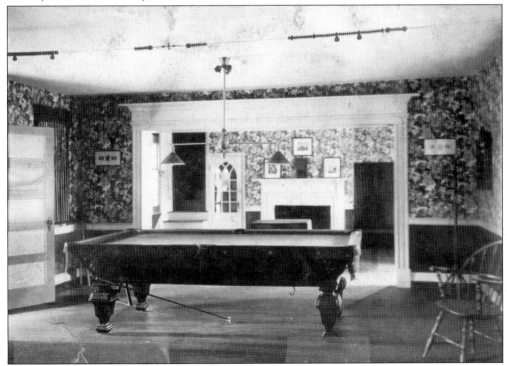

THE EAGLE HOTEL, INTERIOR. Note the wire at ceiling level. What looks like halogen track lighting is, of course, the scorekeeping method for billiards. (Courtesy the Historical Society of Harford County, Inc.)

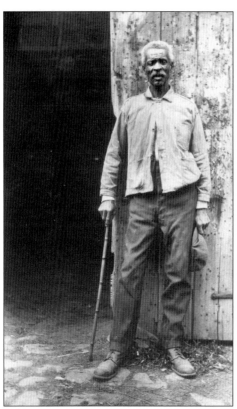

THE EAGLE HOTEL, OLD NED. Ned Taylor's obituary, on page 81, says he could handle 30 teams of horses at a time. If the Eagle had upward of 30 guests at a time, then keeping straight two horses and a carriage was some feat, indeed. (Courtesy the Historical Society of Harford County, Inc.)

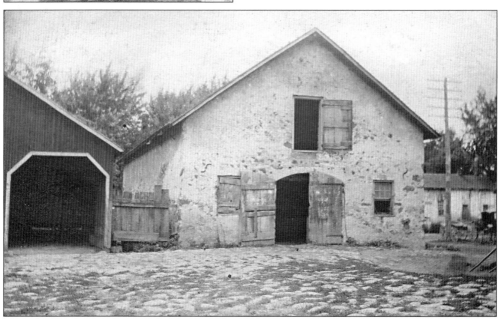

THE EAGLE HOTEL, STABLE. According to Wollen's scrapbook, these are "the stables of the Eagle Hotel 1912 (torn down 1939)." As we have seen, the advent of the automobile eliminated the need for travel by horse, led to paved roads, and changed the face and pace of the small town. (Courtesy the Historical Society of Harford County, Inc.)

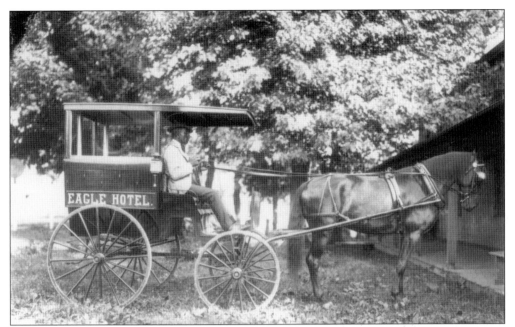

THE EAGLE HOTEL, SHUTTLE CARRIAGE. Visitors came into Bel Air on legal and government business, to sell goods to the town's merchants or buy livestock from the farmers, to pass through on their way to other destinations, and to spend weekends or entire summers away from the heat and smell of the cities. If they arrived by train, this fellow would meet them. (Courtesy the Historical Society of Harford County, Inc.)

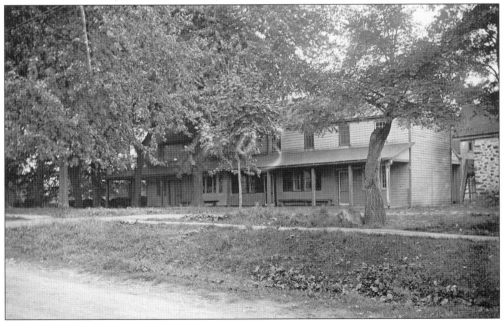

THE COUNTRY CLUB INN. The heyday of the Bel Air hotel is well over. Gone are the Granger, Kenmore, Vaughn, Circle, Yew Tree, and more. The Stagmer is now apartments. There are no hotels within Bel Air town limits. What could take the place of the Country Club Inn? The next photos will show. (Courtesy Gene and Mary Streett, Boyd & Fulford.)

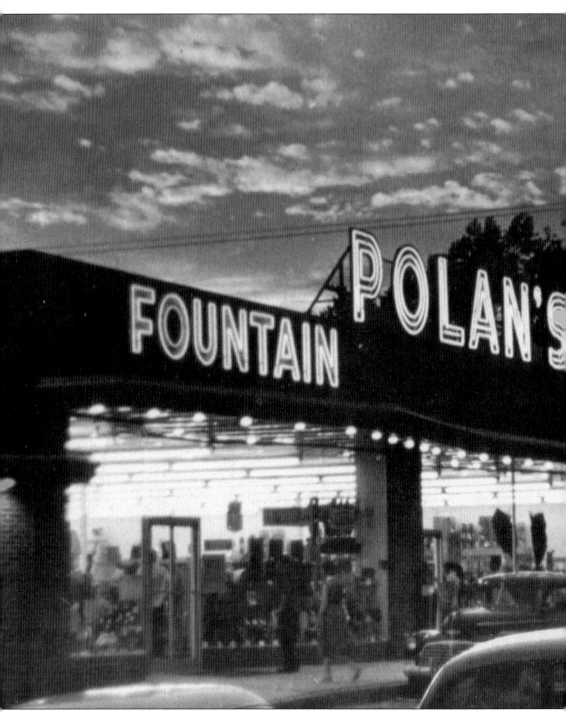

POLAN'S DEPARTMENT STORE. The Country Club Inn gave way to a car dealership, Polan's Department Store, and the A&P. This atmospheric 1940s-era photo by Wayde Chrismer brings out the romance of sky, neon signs, and old cars. The Great Atlantic and Pacific Tea Company, better known as the A&P, was founded in 1859, and it took nearly a century to move from Main Street to Bel Air's first shopping center. But soon it would move even further away to find

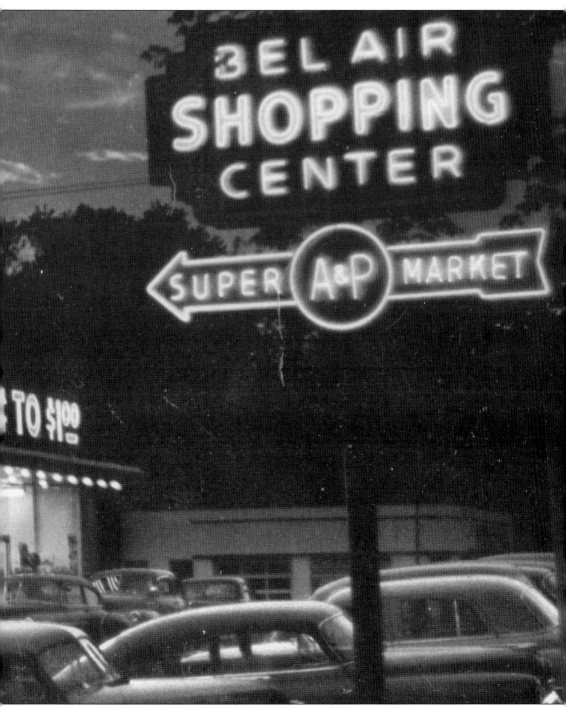

a larger lot and parking galore. Once upon a time, automobiles came in any color, as long as it was black; now Main Street Motor Sales offers more choices, more product lines, and more variety, and had to move to a larger lot on Bond Street, then to a monster lot farther down Route 1. (Courtesy the Historical Society of Harford County, Inc.)

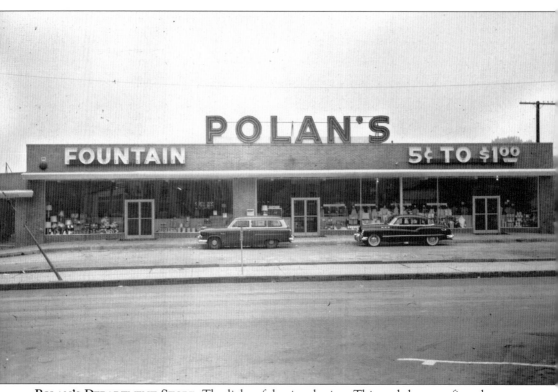

POLAN'S DEPARTMENT STORE. The light of day is sobering. This and the next five photos are from negatives or test prints (with crop marks) by Wayde Chrismer. They are valuable because they shed light on usually unseen portions of Bel Air. The late Chrismer was a Civil War scholar and an amateur photographer in the best sense of the word. (Courtesy the Historical Society of Harford County, Inc.)

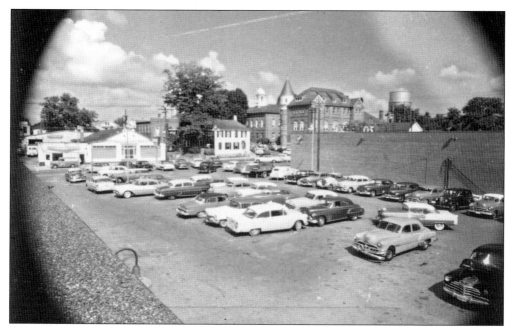

VIEW FROM BOND STREET CAR LOT. In this undated rooftop shot, the big wall on the right is the side of Polan's. Looming large are the water tower, Masonic Temple, and court house. The west end of Office Street opens to Bond Street. A Cities Service gas and service station sits directly across the road from the used car lot. (Courtesy the Historical Society of Harford County, Inc.)

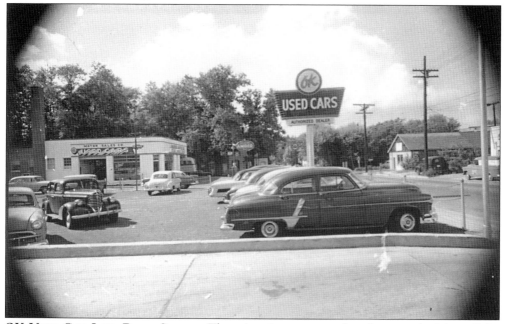

OK USED CAR LOT, BOND STREET. There is quite an array of used cars at the Motor Sales Company. An Amoco gas station sits center in the photo. Everything in the photo is different in 2004. You may find some of the cars, however, at one of the many antique car shows in the area. (Courtesy the Historical Society of Harford County, Inc.)

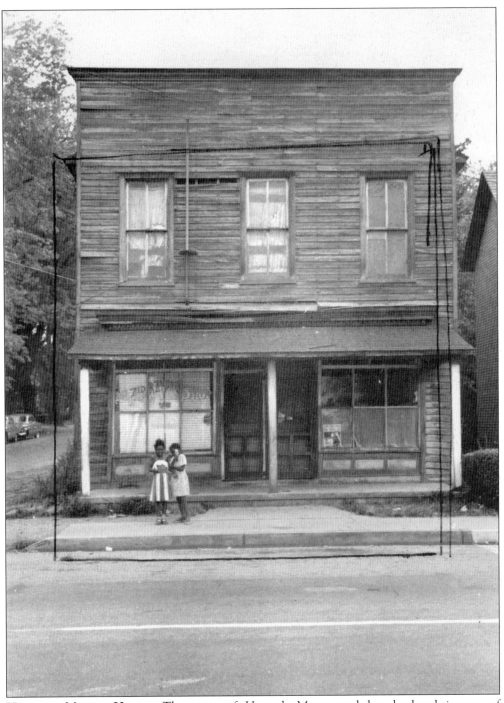

HANNAH MOORE HOUSE. The story of Hannah Moore and her husband is one of determination, hard work, patience, and belief in the power of education. The Moores went from being part of the service workforce to being landowners and millionaires with children in the professions. From the early to the late 1900s, Hannah Moore led (some say ruled) the black community. (Courtesy the Historical Society of Harford County, Inc.)

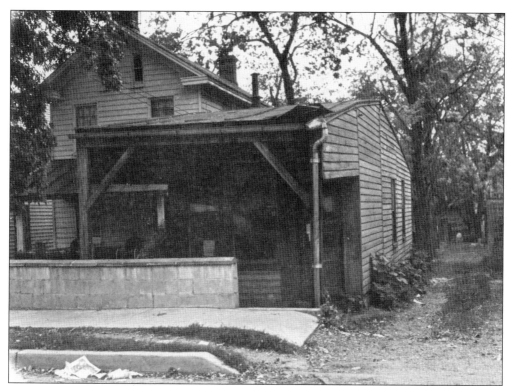

BOND STREET SHOP. This spot is now a town parking lot behind Bond and Thomas Street buildings. Before its commercial development, Bond Street and the area west of it was home to much of Bel Air's black population. Two historic black churches are still in use there. The high school for African Americans was there, as were Hannah Moore's store and recreation center. (Courtesy the Historical Society of Harford County, Inc.)

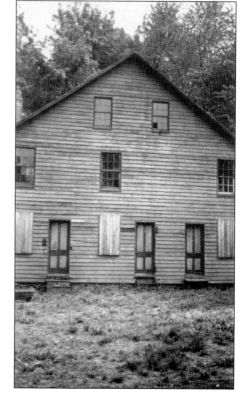

JACOB'S ESTABLISHMENT, ALICEANNE STREET. This building bears a strong resemblance to the Pinckney House on page 21, although it is much larger. It may have been a factory, hotel, or apartment building at one time. (Courtesy the Historical Society of Harford County, Inc.)

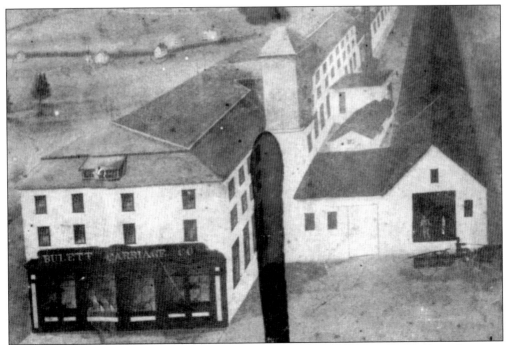

THE BULETT CARRIAGE COMPANY, HAYS STREET. Bel Air was home to a number of carriage makers. The largest must have been Bulett Carriage, founded in 1889. The factory stretched for blocks, from Hays Street to Archer Street east to west, and Thomas Street to Aliceanne Street south to north. The factory held materials for 1,500 carriages with 1,000 in production at any given time. (Courtesy the Historical Society of Harford County, Inc.)

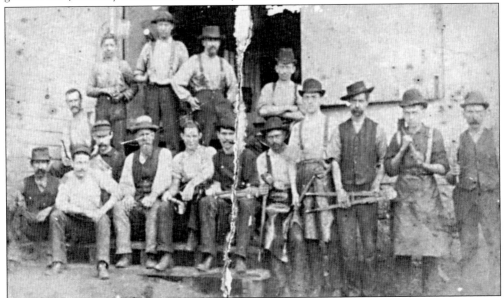

THE BULETT CARRIAGE COMPANY, HAYS STREET. At peak production, the plant employed up to 60 people. Some of the workers are pictured here. They helped to turn out 3,000 carriages a year. These two pictures seem to be the only images of the Bulett factory. (Courtesy the Historical Society of Harford County, Inc.)

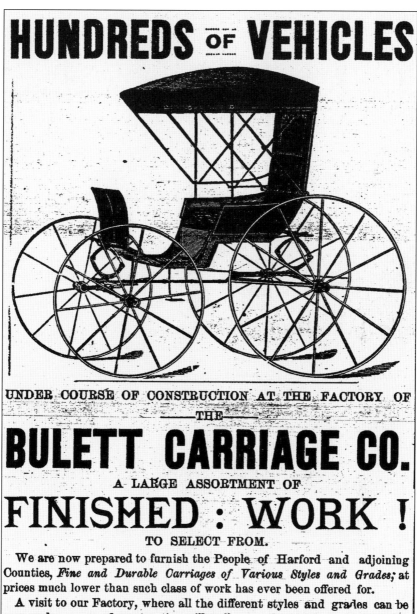

HUNDREDS OF VEHICLES

UNDER COURSE OF CONSTRUCTION AT THE FACTORY OF

THE

BULETT CARRIAGE CO.

A LARGE ASSORTMENT OF

FINISHED : WORK !

TO SELECT FROM.

We are now prepared to furnish the People of Harford and adjoining Counties, *Fine and Durable Carriages of Various Styles and Grades;* at prices much lower than such class of work has ever been offered for.

A visit to our Factory, where all the different styles and grades can be seen under course of construction, will well repay the visitor for his trouble.

BULETT CARRIAGE COMPANY ADVERTISEMENT. In the middle of the night on September 18, 1891, a fire broke out in the Bulett factory, probably in the paint shop. In less than 90 minutes "the most important business enterprise ever undertaken in Bel Air," according to *The Aegis* newspaper, was ashes. The paint, linseed oil, wood, leather, and other materials created such heat that the backdraft from the fire threw off burning chunks and pieces of slate for blocks around. A few nearby houses were kept wet with fire hoses to prevent them from burning. No lives were lost, injuries were few, but up to a dozen Bel Air families had to find homes elsewhere. Neighbors helped save the few carriages from the showroom, and the fire department was praised. Losses were estimated at $90,000 with $47,000 of insurance coverage. (Courtesy Payson Getz.)

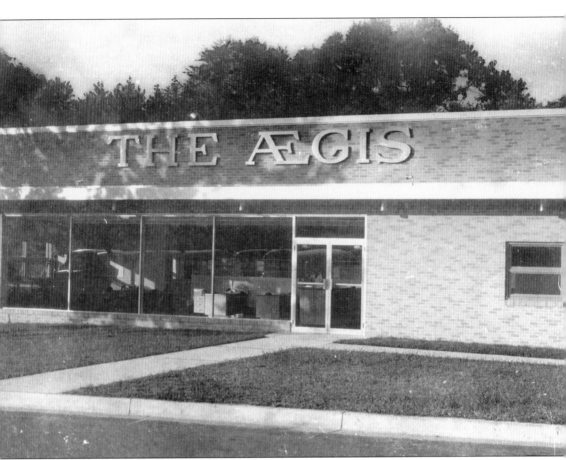

THE *AEGIS* NEWSPAPER BUILDING, HAYS STREET. Since its first newspaper in 1819 Bel Air has seen dozens of publications come and go. *The Aegis* has been in operation since 1856. John D. Worthington bought the paper in 1904 and moved it to 29 Courtland Street. The Hays Street plant, pictured here, opened in 1964 and has recently been remodeled and upgraded. (Courtesy the Historical Society of Harford County, Inc.)

Five

THE EAST SIDE
OF TOWN

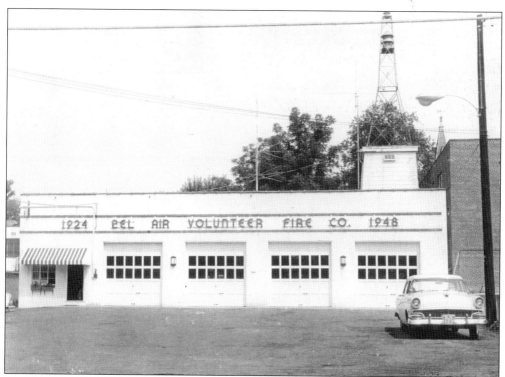

BEL AIR VOLUNTEER FIRE DEPARTMENT. The Bulett Carriage Factory fire of September 18, 1891 (see page 93) was devastating. If not for the bravery and quick work of the fire department, founded just a year earlier, the whole of downtown Bel Air could have been consumed, as so much of downtown Baltimore would be a few years later. (Courtesy the Historical Society of Harford County, Inc.)

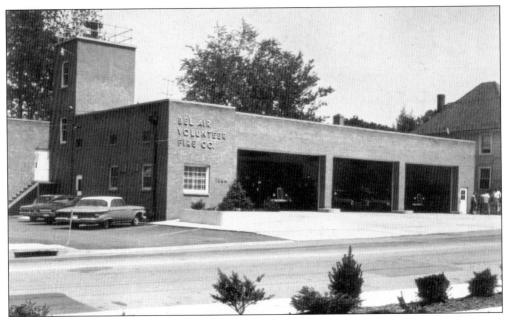

BEL AIR VOLUNTEER FIRE DEPARTMENT. As the town grew, so did the need for more equipment. The Bel Air Volunteer Fire Company, which incorporated in 1924, has moved to several locations, including Bond Street (see page 95). This photo shows its Hickory Avenue location, which has been remodeled recently. The original alarm bell, from the court house, stands outside the new entrance. (Courtesy the Historical Society of Harford County, Inc.)

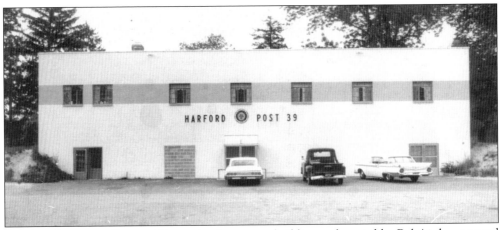

BEL AIR AMERICAN LEGION HALL. As the armory building makes visible, Bel Air has a proud heritage of citizens who have served the nation in wartime. The original American Legion Hall, pictured here, has been expanded to serve the increased number of veterans who have served since the group was chartered in 1929 by the first commander, Louis Getz. (Courtesy the Historical Society of Harford County, Inc.)

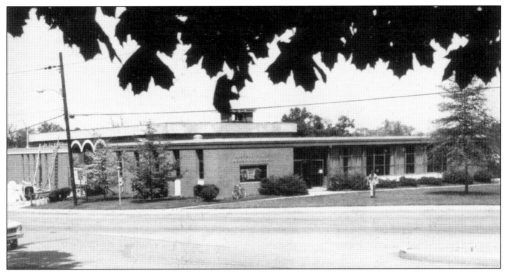

BEL AIR BRANCH, HARFORD COUNTY PUBLIC LIBRARY. After moving around to various locations, including Richardson's Drug Store and the Methodist Protestant Church, the public library settled into its own home on Hickory Avenue in 1959 with additions in 1967. (Courtesy the Historical Society of Harford County, Inc.)

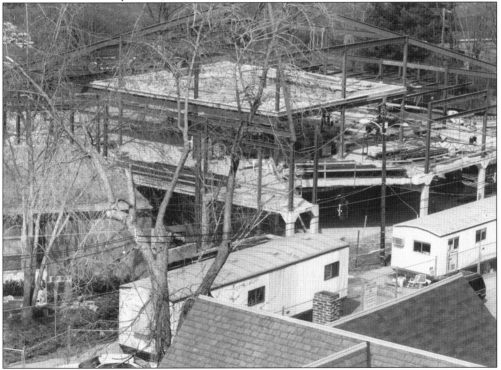

BEL AIR LIBRARY RENOVATION. Over the past decade, a number of facilities in the Harford County Public Library system have been modernized or newly built, bringing new research technologies and other services to all the county's residents. The Bel Air branch was the first to be modernized in the mid-1990s. The aggressive expansion project, seen here, took several years to complete. (Courtesy *The Aegis*.)

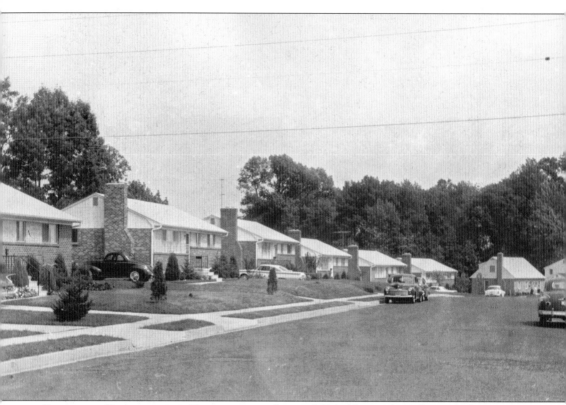

SHAMROCK DEVELOPMENT. From its original size of 42 half-acre plots, the town has grown to its current 2.9 square miles, in large part from estate properties that were turned into residential developments. One such development is the Shamrock area, named for Shamrock, the home of the Archer family and previously the home of the Bel Air Academy's first principal, Rev. Reuben Davis. (Courtesy the Historical Society of Harford County, Inc.)

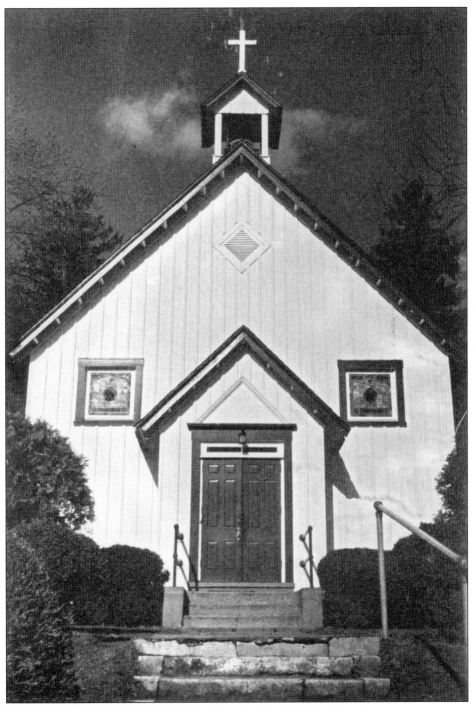

SAINT MARGARET CHURCH. Bel Air's Roman Catholic parish, Saint Margaret, has expanded several times from the original 1905 church (pictured here and is now used as a chapel). The 1969 church was augmented a few years ago by the creation of a satellite parish, St. Mary Magdalene, which includes a middle school to complement Saint Margaret's elementary school. (Courtesy the Historical Society of Harford County, Inc.)

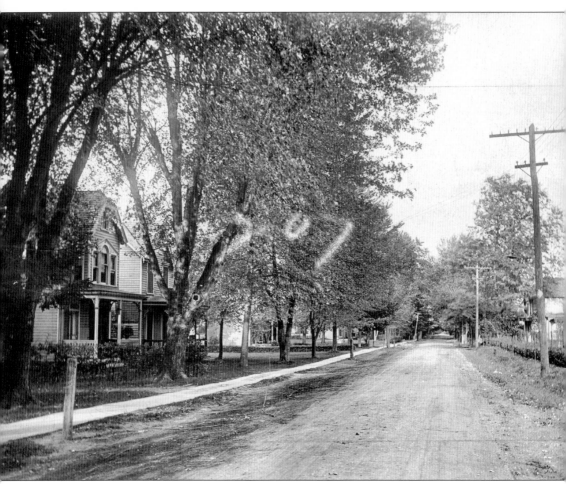

VIEW OF BROADWAY. This is a photo proof for a postcard looking east on Broadway, which was solely residential. Hannah Moore recalls friends earning up to $2.50 per day for working in the home of Broadway's professionals, especially lawyers. Today many of the homes have been converted into offices. Several of the larger homes have been transformed into nursing homes. (Courtesy Gene and Mary Streett, Boyd & Fulford.)

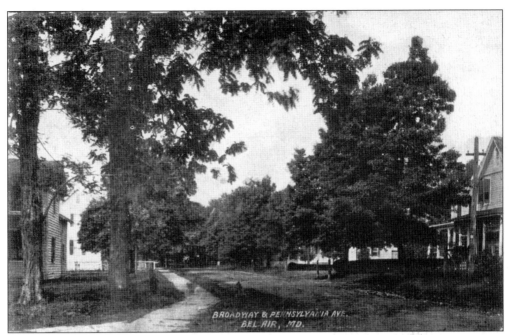

VIEW OF BROADWAY AND PENNSYLVANIA AVENUE. Today's Broadway and Pennsylvania are roughly parallel. However, before the 1933 sewer improvements, Pennsylvania made a curve onto what is today called Hickory Avenue and then intersected Broadway as Hickory does today. Actually, stretches of Hickory Avenue have had a number of different names, including Residence Street and Dallam Place. (Courtesy the Historical Society of Harford County, Inc.)

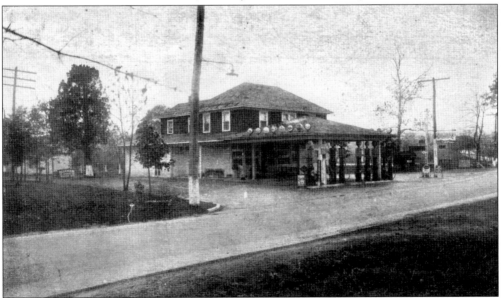

DEL HAVEN CAMP. The Del Haven Hotel and Cottages stood on the northwest corner of Route 1 and Moore's Mill Road and was famous for having the first public swimming pool in Bel Air. According to Felicia Jackson, before the recreation features and cottages were developed, there stood a gas station, restaurant, and campground, as seen in this postcard photo. (Courtesy the Historical Society of Harford County, Inc.)

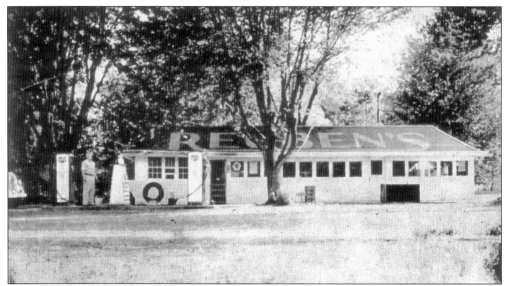

REUBEN'S DRIVE-IN. Recalling his days at the new Bel Air High School, which opened in 1951, Dennis Baxter points to Reuben's as the place guys went to hang out before and after a hot date. To impress a girl, a young man would take her into Baltimore, maybe to the Stanley or Hippodrome Theaters or, for a real dreamboat, on a Harbor Cruise. (Courtesy the Historical Society of Harford County, Inc.)

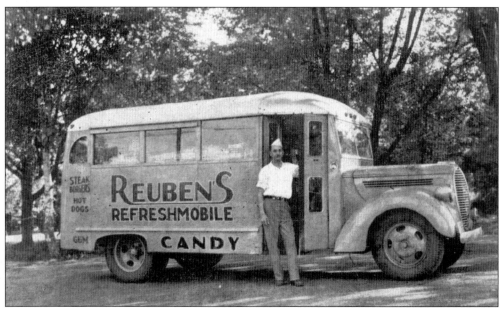

REUBEN'S REFRESHMOBILE. Reuben Leftwich took his steakburgers, Suzy-Qs, and double thick milk shakes to the road. Dennis Baxter recalls that if a customer asked for a hamburger and fries, Reuben wouldn't serve him or her. A customer had to ask for a steakburger and Suzy-Qs, Reuben's version of curly fries. (Courtesy the Historical Society of Harford County, Inc.)

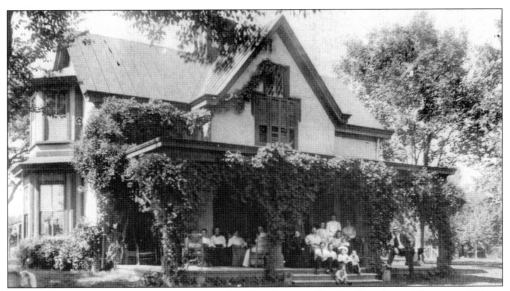

TUDOR HALL. This was the American home of Junius Brutus Booth and his sons Edwin and John. The home, always privately owned, was originally brick, and then, at some point, it was covered in stucco. The folks in this photo are later residents. The house, in need of repair, was auctioned off to a couple who have remodeled it. (Courtesy the Historical Society of Harford County, Inc.)

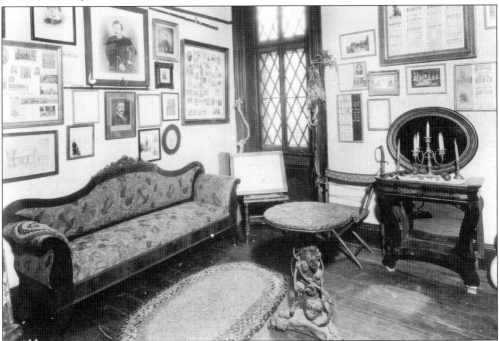

TUDOR HALL, INTERIOR. This undated photo shows a museum room at Tudor Hall filled with Booth memorabilia. Are the items authentic? Notice the pipe and spur on John's portrait. Tudor Hall was a major stop for folks following the Lincoln history trail. The Booth brothers were born in Harford County and, according to local legend, John was a solitary and troubled child. (Courtesy the Historical Society of Harford County, Inc.)

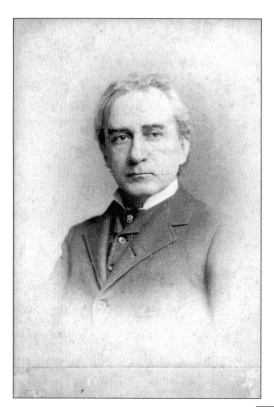

EDWIN BOOTH. On the back of this photo is written, "Edwin Booth Present Age, Bel Air Aug 29, 1889." Edwin's reputation as a great Shakespearean actor was treasured by the community. When his portrait was placed in the Bel Air Court House, the tradition began of placing portraits of other great local notables there. (Courtesy the Historical Society of Harford County, Inc.)

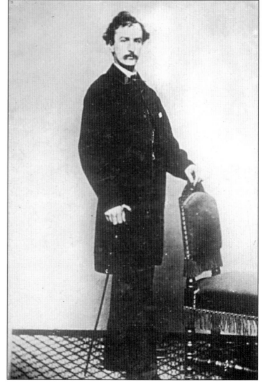

JOHN WILKES BOOTH. John was the only Presidential assassin born in Harford County. He grew up with an alcoholic father who had another wife and family in England. John's older brother was adored locally and around the world as a distinguished actor. John tried an acting career, but chose another path to fame as Abraham Lincoln's murderer. (Courtesy the Historical Society of Harford County, Inc.)

Six

THE WEST SIDE OF TOWN

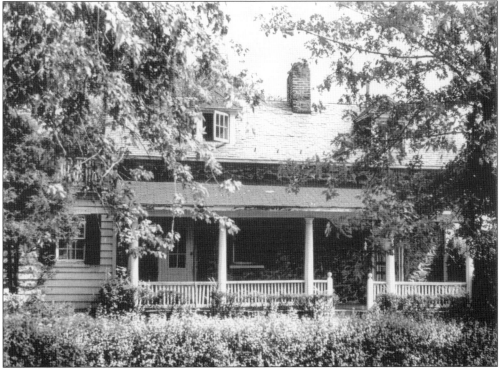

THE TOLL HOUSE. This stone house sat at Tollgate Road and Route 1 by Harford Mall. After 1849, people using the paved Bel Air Turnpike would pay when going past the toll house, depending on the type of vehicle and what they were carrying: 6¢ for 20 hogs or sheep, double that for 20 cattle, 4¢ per horse and rider, etc. (Courtesy the Historical Society of Harford County, Inc.)

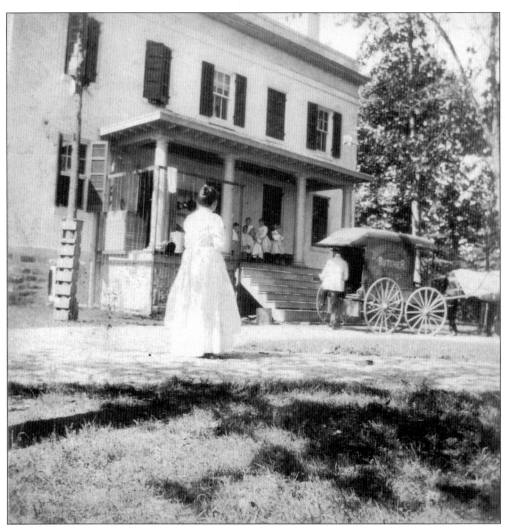

LIRIODENDRON MANSION. Known as the Kelly House, the Kelly Place, or the Kelly Mansion, the home and grounds were collectively named Liriodendron by the owner, Dr. Howard Kelly. The name is Latin for a kind of tree with tulip-like flowers. Dr. Kelly, a world-famous gynecologist, began the Johns Hopkins Hospital with a team of doctors of differing specialties. They were known as the "Big Four" and changed the way medicine was practiced in the hospital setting. Dr. Kelly built Liriodendron as a summer retreat from his Bolton Hill home in Baltimore to get away from the heat and smell of the city. He modeled the house after the style of his wife Laetitia's childhood home in Germany because she had been homesick, not that their nine children left her much time for herself. In the photo, Joseph Coale delivers meat to the back entrance of Liriodendron from his Main Street store. Some of the children are on the porch. (Courtesy the Liriodendron Foundation.)

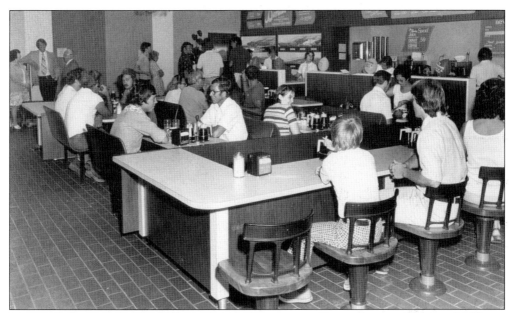

MERRY-O DONUT SHOP. Coffee was 20¢ a cup, juice 30¢ a glass, and donuts $1.59 per dozen. This photo is from the early 1970s, when Charles Lutz rented land on the north end of Baltimore Pike to Merry-O and Burger King. The King still rules, but Merry-O's 59¢ breakfast special is long gone. In 2004, La Tolteca, a Mexican restaurant, is located there. (Courtesy Charles L. Lutz, Inc.)

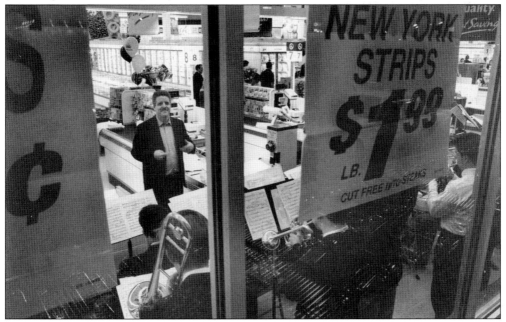

SUPERFRESH REMODELING, 1995. In the 1960s, Safeway cleared away the Kenmore Inn and Hays House to build in the heart of town. The developers of Bel Air Plaza built instead on the outskirts of town. The A&P moved there to accommodate its ever-increasing food selection and morphed into SuperFresh later. Don McClure of the Bel Air High School stage band directs at a remodeling celebration. (Courtesy *The Aegis*.)

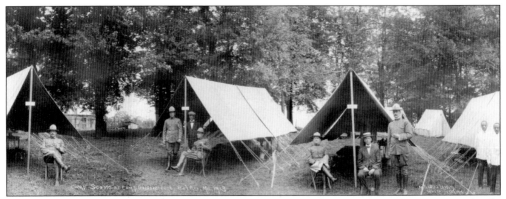

CAMP GOLDSBOROUGH, 1913. In 1913, as the country made preparations for war, Maryland's Gov. Phillips Lee Goldsborough (in office from 1912 to 1916, pictured here in straw hat and civvies) visited local troops training at Camp Goldsborough, located on Baltimore Pike across from the Bel Air Race Track, where Tollgate Plaza is today. This and the next photo were taken with a special panoramic camera. (Courtesy the Historical Society of Harford County, Inc.)

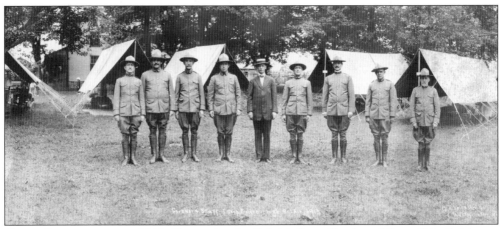

CAMP GOLDSBOROUGH, 1913. Except for the Bel Air Race Track and Farm Fair, Baltimore Pike remained largely farm and residential until the late 1940s. When Clyde Grove moved Grove's Plumbing and Heating to the Pike in 1947, Dennis Baxter recalls, the only other business there was a huge lumber yard that went from the Pike back for several blocks. (Courtesy the Historical Society of Harford County, Inc.)

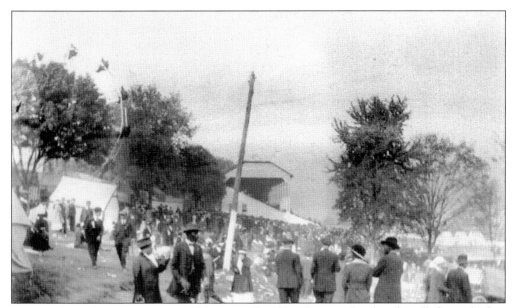

Bel Air Fair Grounds, 1920s. The county fair, like the state fair, has dwindled to a shadow of its former self when agriculture, as the lifeblood of the economy, more directly affected people's everyday lives. Notice the Bel Air Race Track grandstand in the background. Blacks and whites owned and trained race horses, and racing is still a vital piece of Harford's economy. (Courtesy the Historical Society of Harford County, Inc.)

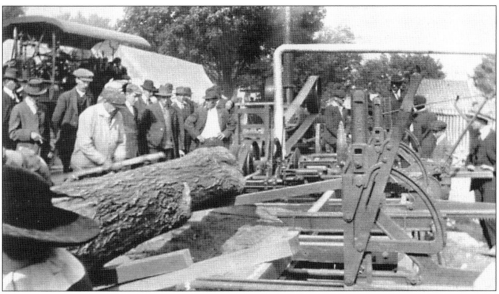

Bel Air Fair Grounds, 1920s. At a time when mechanization was beginning to change farming, some farmers, like James Walls, would continue with the traditional horse and plow for planting and the scythe for reaping years after the introduction of motor-driven farm machines, such as the log cutters being demonstrated in this photo. (Courtesy the Historical Society of Harford County, Inc.)

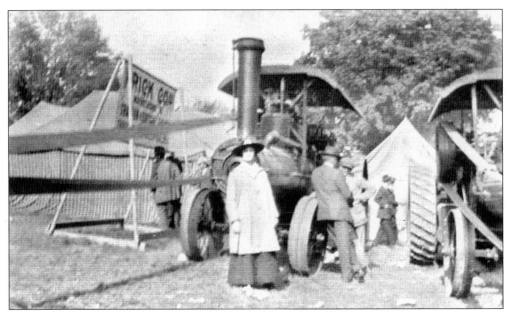

BEL AIR FAIR GROUNDS, 1920s. The first tractors were driven by steam engines. Notice the giant belt on the tractor on the right that powered the tractor's accessories. People must have oohed and aahed at the contraptions, much as residents do today at the line of giant John Deere equipment at the Farm Fair. (Courtesy the Historical Society of Harford County, Inc.)

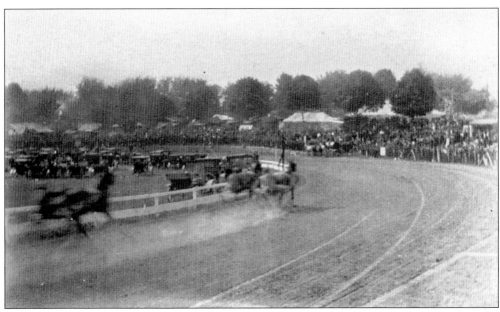

BEL AIR RACE TRACK, 1920s. The Bel Air Race Track was one of a group of Maryland tracks, including Laurel, Havre de Grace, Pimlico, and Timonium. During its existence from the late 1800s to the 1960s, improvements were made to the track and grand stand to keep pace with the times and crowds. (Courtesy the Historical Society of Harford County, Inc.)

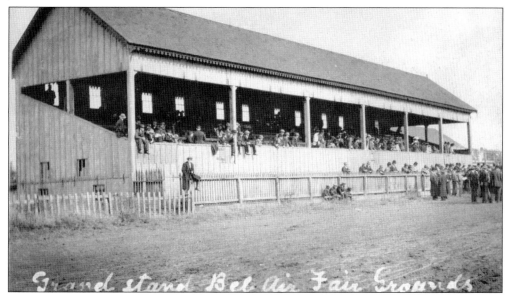

BEL AIR RACE TRACK, GRAND STAND, UNDATED. In 1962, the racing and fairs came to an end. Over the years, attendance at had dropped; he attractiveness of profit from developing the land as retail space outweighed the popularity of the races. In the mid-1970s, land became available from the sale to Harford County the Liriodendron Estate by Fritz Kelly. Part of the land was used as a permanent site for the Harford County Farm Fair as the Bel Air Equestrian Center. Since then the fair has run every year in late July or early August, from a Thursday to a Sunday. The heart of the fair still revolves around agricultural-related activities, such as 4H judging, tractor pulls, pig races, and barnyard animal imitation contests. The variety of animals on show is probably the best it has ever been, from llamas and Vietnamese pot-bellied pigs to long-eared rabbits and pygmy goats. (Courtesy the Historical Society of Harford County, Inc.)

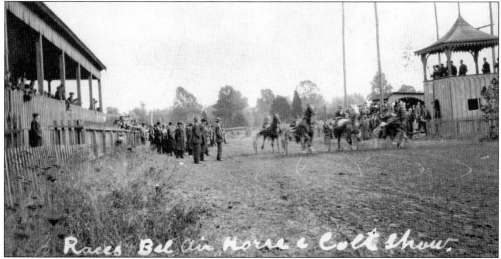

BEL AIR RACE TRACK: RACES, BEL AIR HORSE AND COLT SHOW, UNDATED. The horse industry is still a vibrant part of Harford's fame worldwide. Among locally bred legends is Cigar, who was born in 1990 at Country Life Farm, earned almost $10 million over his career, and was the first horse to tie Citation's record of 16 straight wins. (Courtesy the Historical Society of Harford County, Inc.)

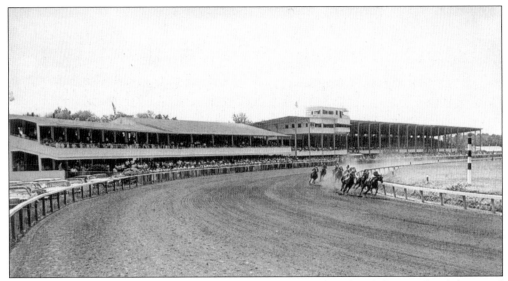

BEL AIR RACE TRACK. Over the years, the race track was widened and elongated and the grand stand was enlarged considerably. Of course, the Bel Air hotels could accommodate visitors. This photo is from the late 1950s or early 1960s near the end of the race track's run. (Courtesy the Historical Society of Harford County, Inc.)

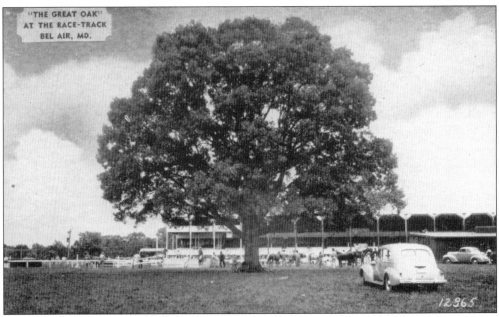

BEL AIR RACE TRACK, OAK TREE. Local lore has it that two women chained themselves to the great oak when the race track was being demolished. The county has its proponents of change and its proponents of the natural status quo. Perhaps the tension between these forces helps the county keep much of its country beauty while maintaining itself as a bedroom community. (Courtesy the Historical Society of Harford County, Inc.)

112

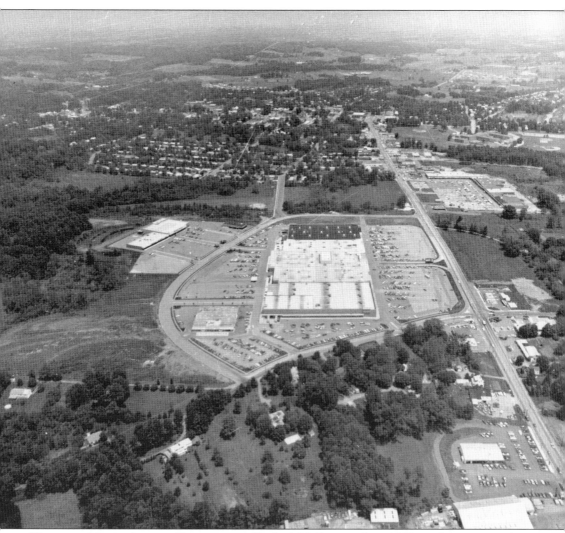

HARFORD MALL, AERIAL VIEW, 1972. Harford Mall opened in 1972, and it remains the county's only enclosed shopping facility. In this photo, the mall is center, fronting on Baltimore Pike (Route 1). Parking surrounds the mall. Bel Air Shopping Plaza sits to the upper right. Behind the mall are two large, low buildings, the rightmost of which is a Pantry Pride food store. Still noticeably missing is Route 24, which would boost shopping space development, most notably Tollgate Plaza, the Festival at Bel Air, the Constant Friendship shopping area, and the area near the intersection of Route 24 and I-95. (Courtesy the Historical Society of Harford County, Inc.)

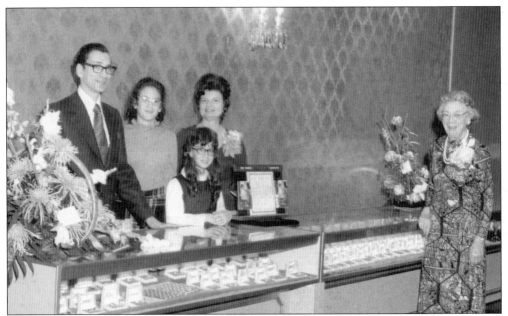

HARFORD MALL, GETZ JEWELERS, 1972. Simon Getz opened his jewelry and gift shop on Main Street in 1936. Simon's wife, Kate, and son, Payson, moved the shop to Harford Mall in 1972. Later Main Street would call him back. Payson retired and sold his business to employee Marcus Johnston. Pictured are, from left to right, the following: Payson Getz, Susan Getz, Ellen Getz, Elaine Getz, and Kate Getz. (Courtesy Payson Getz.)

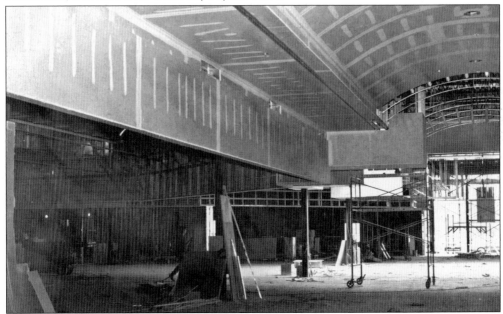

HARFORD MALL, FOOD COURT CONSTRUCTION. With the ever-growing population, Harford Mall has expanded several times since 1972. The addition of a food court made the facility more competitive with other malls in the area. In the photo, light streams in from the huge windows, which will front onto Baltimore Pike. Skylights and new entrances will also flood the space with light. (Courtesy the Historical Society of Harford County, Inc.)

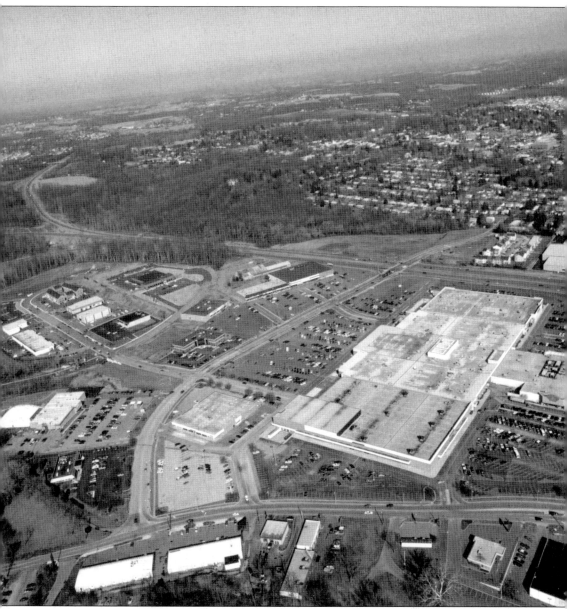

HARFORD MALL, AERIAL VIEW. Harford Mall's food court extension is on the right of the photo. Behind the mall are Pantry Pride and a strip shopping center. Boulton Street runs behind the mall. The Parris-Castoro Eye Center and the beginnings of the Bel Air Athletic Club are visible at the intersection of Boulton Street and Gateway Drive. Further back on Gateway is the office park, including Musicland and Arrow Lighting. The mall aspires to be Main Street, a place for everyone in town to gather, to be entertained, to shop. Just as, at one time, families could do all their holiday shopping in one trip up and down Main Street in Bel Air, so the mall tries to replace that experience under one roof. However, the indoor mall is giving way to new trends. The Avenue at White Marsh is an attempt to re-create Main Street outdoors. The Hunt Valley Mall has demolished the small shops under its roof in favor of huge stores and restaurants on pad sites. (Courtesy the Historical Society of Harford County, Inc.)

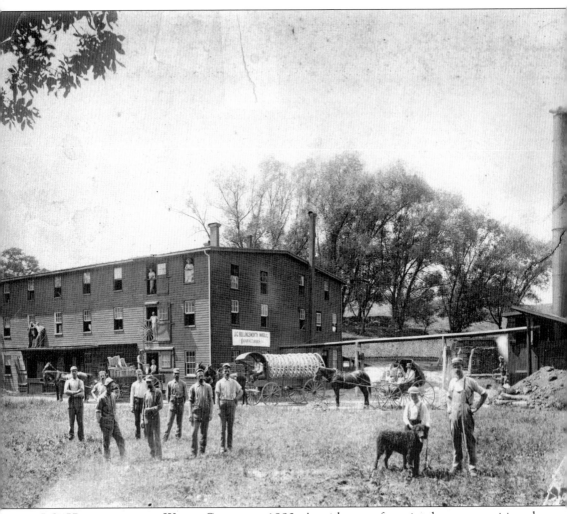

J.C. HOLLINGSWORTH WHEEL COMPANY, 1893. As with many factories that were positioned by water to run the machinery of the shop, this wheel factory was situated on Winters Run. The building of the Atkinson Dam by the water company led to the flooding of this area. The level of detail in this photo, despite its age and condition, is on a par with the best photos in this book. Things to notice include: the wagon load of wagon wheels at the center of the photo; to the right of the wagon is a horse-drawn carriage with a woman and four children, presumably Joel Hollingsworth's family; the man and boy with a dog in the right foreground may be Hollingsworth himself with another of his sons. The group of men in the left foreground, scattered and in casual poses, complements the men in the background at the factory doorways, loading supplies, and looking out windows. (Courtesy the Historical Society of Harford County, Inc.)

Seven
TRANSPORTATION

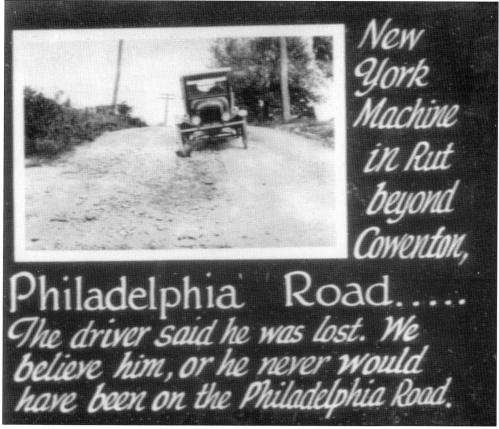

PROMOTIONAL AD FOR PHILADELPHIA ROAD IMPROVEMENTS. This image is from a series of silent movie theater ads designed to drum up funding to pave Philadelphia Road (Route 7). This would expedite the development of Edgewood Arsenal and the heavy equipment that needed to be transported. (Courtesy the Historical Society of Harford County, Inc.)

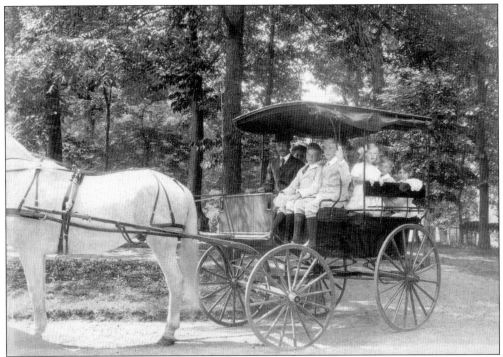

HORSE AND CARRIAGE, LIRIODENDRON, 1907. The nine Kelly children living at their summer home, Liriodendron, preferred the outdoors for play. Often they would go into town, pulled in their "wagonette" by their horse Beauty. Pictured are, from left to right, the following: Mr. Thomas, the coachman; Esther; Howdy; Fritz; Titia; Bully; and Margy Kelly. (Courtesy the Liriodendron Foundation.)

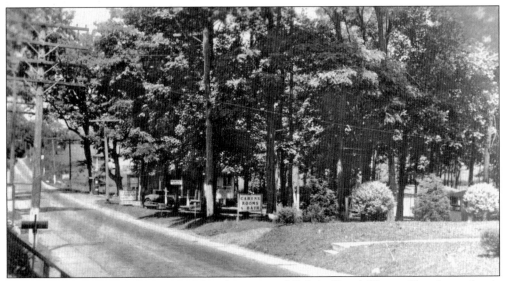

CONCRETE SHOULDERS, ROUTE 1. Macadam covered Bel Air Road (Route 1) early on, but it needed frequent repair. The addition of concrete shoulders to the road added stability and allowed rain to roll off the road more readily. Macadam was named for its inventor, the Scot Mac Adam. (Courtesy the Historical Society of Harford County, Inc.)

118

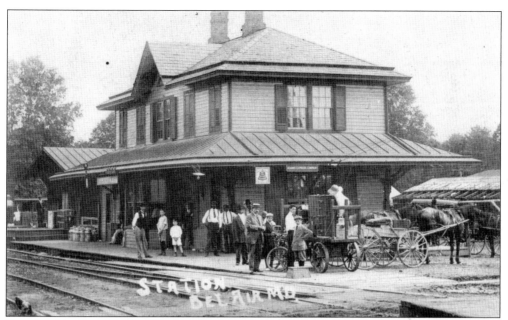

BEL AIR TRAIN STATION, 1911. The Ma & Pa Line, short for Maryland and Pennsylvania, was one of the nation's interconnecting train lines, linking the residents of small towns such as Bel Air to other towns and cities throughout the country. The Bel Air Station was at the north end of Main Street and stayed in use until the 1960s. (Courtesy the Historical Society of Harford County, Inc.)

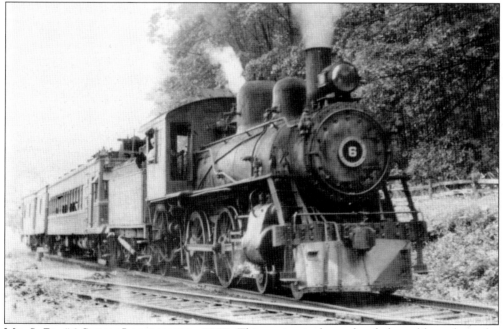

MA & PA #6 STEAM LOCOMOTIVE, 1947. This engine is shown headed northbound. As the interstates were built, allowing for faster transport of goods by truck and allowing people to motor to central stations, trains stopped going to small towns but instead linked cities to cities. (Courtesy the Historical Society of Harford County, Inc.)

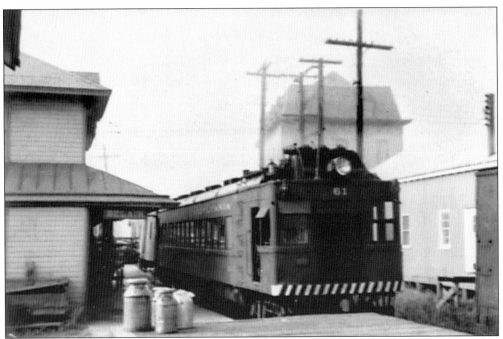

MA & PA MOTOR #61 NORTHBOUND, 1951. The train is stopped at Bel Air Station (on left) with Southern States (Reckord Mill) looming in the background on the right. Trains carried people, milk collected from area farms for shipping to Baltimore, produce from farms, and goods from canneries. (Courtesy the Historical Society of Harford County, Inc.)

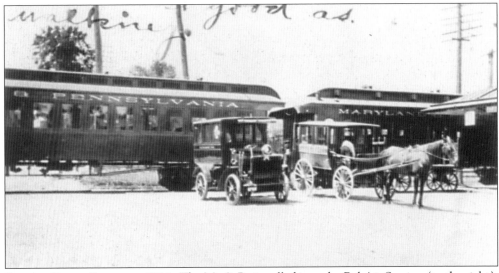

BEL AIR TRAIN STATION, 1911. The Ma & Pa is pulled into the Bel Air Station (to the right). Two familiar sights greet visitors: the horse and carriage from the Eagle Hotel (on the right) and the horseless carriage from the Kenmore Inn (left). Writing on the photo attests to the comfort level in those days: "This isn't as good as walking." (Courtesy the Historical Society of Harford County, Inc.)

Eight

SCHOOLS AND SPORTS

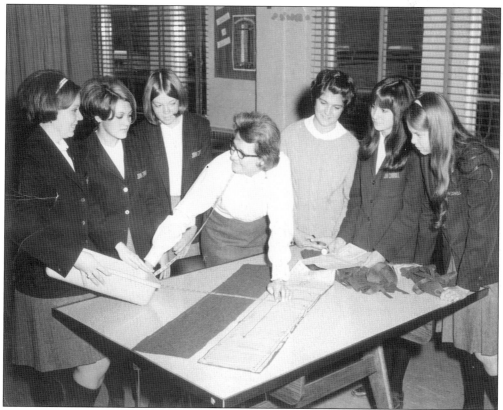

JOHN CARROLL SCHOOL, HOME ECONOMICS CLASS, 1970. Ellen Sitter teaches John Carroll ladies about sewing patterns. John Carroll, the county's Catholic high school, was founded in 1964 as a coed school, providing Harford students an alternative to single-sex Catholic high schools in Baltimore. (Courtesy John Carroll School.)

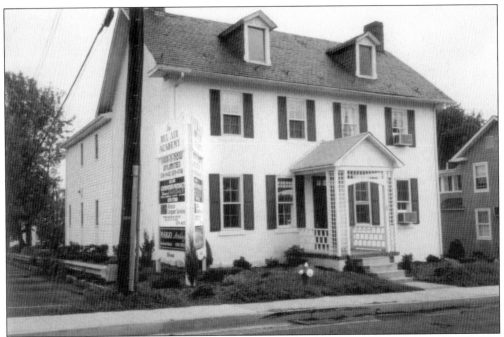

BEL AIR ACADEMY. Bel Air's first school, the Academy, was founded in 1811 and settled by 1815 into the building pictured. Early on, the original stone was plastered over. The first principal, Rev. Reuben Davis, was fond of maintaining discipline by caning his students; he kept a stock of rods behind his seat. (Courtesy the Historical Society of Harford County, Inc.)

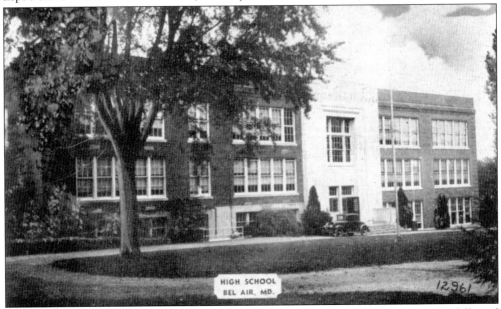

BEL AIR HIGH SCHOOL. A public one-room schoolhouse was built in Bel Air in 1870, followed by a graded school. By 1924 the elementary and high school had to split to accommodate the number of students. The Bel Air High School, pictured, was the result and was considered the "new" high school until the current "new" one was opened in 1950. (Courtesy the Historical Society of Harford County, Inc.)

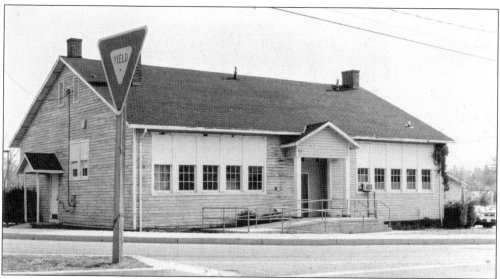

BEL AIR COLORED HIGH SCHOOL. In 1883, the one-room schoolhouse was moved to Hays Street to use as a school for African-American children, and in 1924 a new building was added. By 1935, the high school grades were added to the elementary grades. The school closed in 1950, when the Central Consolidated School in Hickory was to open the next school year. (Courtesy the Historical Society of Harford County, Inc.)

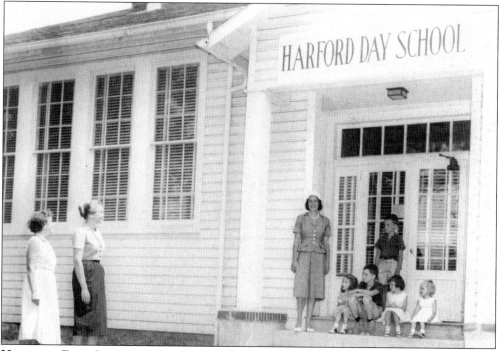

HARFORD DAY SCHOOL. Like the Bel Air Academy, Harford Day School is a private elementary school, but that is where the similarities end. Located on the outskirts of town on Moore's Mill Road, the school has expanded several times and has separate buildings for pre-school and kindergarten, elementary, and middle school grades. (Courtesy the Historical Society of Harford County, Inc.)

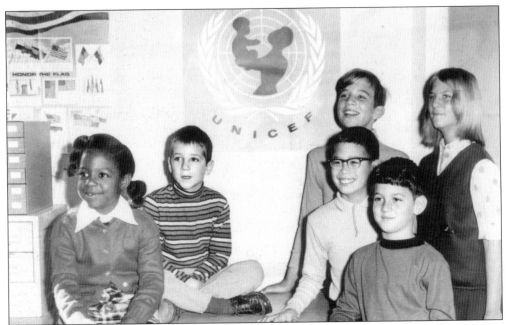

HARFORD DAY SCHOOL STUDENTS. Harford Day students celebrate their successful UNICEF collection. Maria Terry is on the left; other students are unidentified. As an adult, Maria continues to contribute as an active member of the Harford community and as a business owner. (Courtesy the Historical Society of Harford County, Inc.)

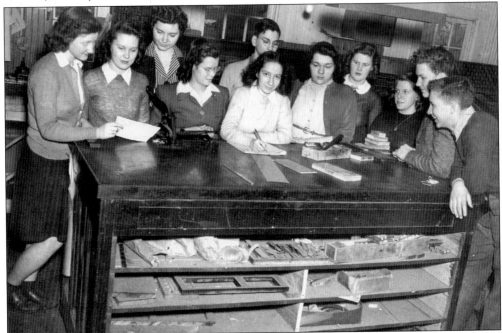

BEL AIR HIGH, *THE BELAIRION*, 1945. Bel Air High School's newspaper staff, pictured in the office of *The Aegis*, included from left to right, Grace Archer; Lillian Archer; Miss ? Walker; teacher; Payson Getz; Doris Everett; Molly Coppel; Betty Getz; Ruth Magness; unidentified; Ira Zepp; and Stanley Alexander. (Courtesy Payson Getz.)

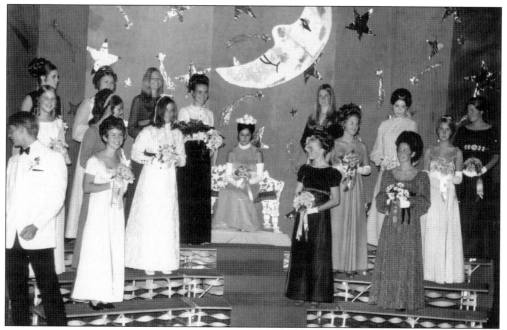

BEL AIR HIGH, AUTUMN COURT. Contrast this undated photo with the photo below. The styles vary widely from today's, showing that the only thing that is sure is change. (Courtesy the Historical Society of Harford County, Inc.)

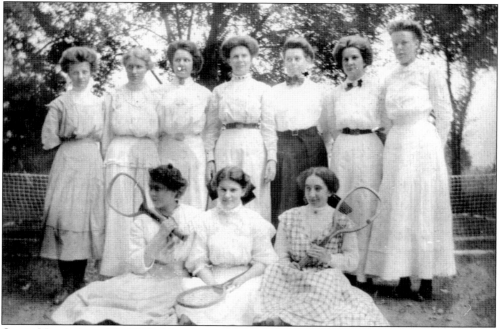

CLASS NO. 6, JULY 13, 1909. Here is a mystery: all the details are written on the photo, except the name of the school. Pictured are, from left to right, the following: (front row, seated) Beatrice Harkins, Inez Scarff, and Christie Enfield; (back row) Edna Walbeck, Margaret Robinson, Bessie Walbeck, Cousin Sally Harkins, Laura England, Annie Walbeck, and Mary Cloman. (Courtesy the Historical Society of Harford County, Inc.)

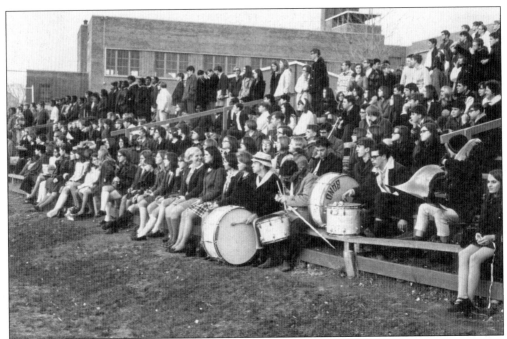

BEL AIR HIGH SCHOOL. Bel Air High seniors cheer on the team. Sports are often an important element in high school life, but Bel Air really supports its teams. Up to 5,000 fans attended Bel Air High football games in the 1950s under Coach Al Cesky. (Courtesy the Historical Society of Harford County, Inc.)

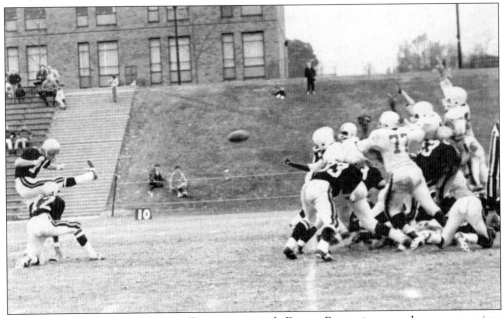

JOHN CARROLL SCHOOL. Al Neville teams up with Danny Bungori to put three more points on the scoreboard for John Carroll in their big win over Northern (Baltimore). In the years before C. Milton Wright High School opened, the John Caroll-Bel Air High football match ups were legendary. (Courtesy the Historical Society of Harford County, Inc.)

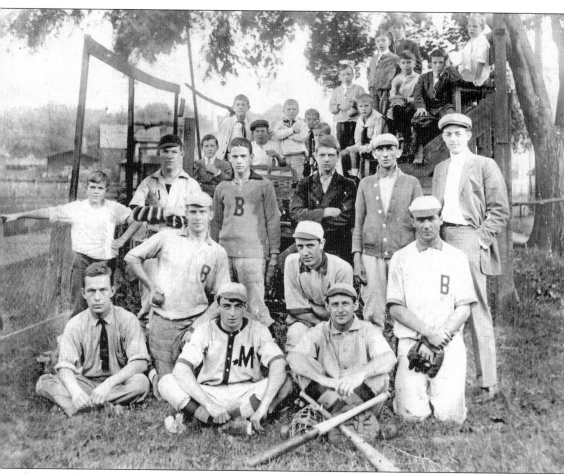

BEL AIR BASEBALL TEAM, 1900. Bel Air took to baseball almost instantly; long before 1900 the town had a fully developed group of young men playing such teams as the Aberdeen Canners as part of the amateur Susquehanna League. John Schafer recalled his favorite activity as a young man: to break the long hours of school and work at his father's garage, John loved going to the lot at Del Haven to play ball. Just as when many of us were growing up, you only needed a ball, a bat, and a bunch of guys and you had a great pick up game. But baseball was more than just fun; members of the Bel Air team formed a solidarity and familiarity that influenced their roles as their generation's civic leaders. Pictured from left to right are the following: (first row) Edward Hollingsworth, Lloyd Richardson, and Dick Bode; (second row) Harry Webb, unidentified, and Hal Calder; (third row) Herb Webb, John Hunter, Albert Johnston, Dick Richardson, Jimmie Carroll, and John Richardson; (fourth row) Henry Bruns, unidentified, Shorty Cahill, Zack Debow, two unidentified, ? Debow, Bob Richardson, John Webster, Buck Richardson, Bill Nelson, Dick Dallam, Joe Carroll, and Ned Webster. (Courtesy the Historical Society of Harford County, Inc.)

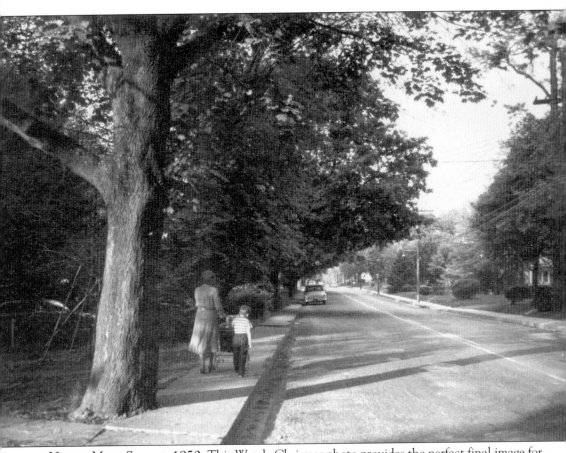

NORTH MAIN STREET, 1950. This Wayde Chrismer photo provides the perfect final image for this book. Sunlight shines on the tree in the foreground, bringing out the texture of the bark, making the warmth visible. As they stroll up Main Street, a mother (the photographer's wife, Catherine), her child, and her baby in the carriage begin to blend into the cool of the long shadows of the trees that line the street. The noise and usual bustle of business seem far away down the road with few cars. It is a quiet moment, the kind of quiet many come to Bel Air hoping to find. The quiet is still there in an evening stroll, on weekends. It's there in memory and in images such as these. But remember, from its beginning, Bel Air was made for growth and change. You can continue your exploration of the Bel Air of yesterday and today at www.belairbook.com. (Courtesy the Historical Society of Harford County, Inc.)